OECD Economic Surveys:
South Africa
2013

OECD

BETTER POLICIES FOR BETTER LIVES

This document and any map included herein are without prejudice to the status of or sovereignty over any territory, to the delimitation of international frontiers and boundaries and to the name of any territory, city or area.

Please cite this publication as:

OECD (2013), *OECD Economic Surveys: South Africa 2013*, OECD Publishing.
http://dx.doi.org/10.1787/eco_surveys-zaf-2013-en

ISBN 978-92-64-18230-1 (print)
ISBN 978-92-64-18232-5 (PDF)

Series: OECD Economic Surveys
ISSN 0376-6438 (print)
ISSN 1609-7513 (online)

OECD Economic Surveys: South Africa
ISSN 2218-6131 (print)
ISSN 2218-614X (online)

The statistical data for Israel are supplied by and under the responsibility of the relevant Israeli authorities. The use of such data by the OECD is without prejudice to the status of the Golan Heights, East Jerusalem and Israeli settlements in the West Bank under the terms of international law.

Photo credit: Cover © Shutterstock/Sean Nel.

Corrigenda to OECD publications may be found on line at: *www.oecd.org/publishing/corrigenda*.

Table of contents

Tables

Figures

This Survey was prepared in the Economics Department by Geoff Barnard and Fabrice Murtin under the supervision of Andreas Wörgötter. The draft has benefited from valuable background research by Yaseen Jhaveri, seconded from the South African National Treasury. Research assistance was provided by Corinne Chanteloup and secretarial assistance by Josiane Gutierrez and Pascal Halim. The Survey also benefited from valuable background research by Nicola Branson and Murray Leibbrandt from SALDRU at the University of Cape Town, and by George Frempong, Dean Janse van Rensburg, Vijay Reddy and Lolita Winnaar from the Human Sciences Research Council.

The Economic Survey of South Africa was discussed by the Economic Development and Review Committee on 17 December 2012, with active participation of representatives of the South African government .

This Survey is published under the responsibility of the Secretary-General of the OECD.

The previous Economic Survey of South Africa was issued in July 2010.

Information about the latest as well as previous Surveys and more information about how Surveys are prepared is available at www.oecd.org/eco/surveys.

BASIC STATISTICS OF SOUTH AFRICA, 2011

(The numbers in parentheses refer to the OECD average)

LAND, PEOPLE AND ELECTORAL CYCLE

Population (1 000 000):	50.7		Population density per km²	41.3	(34.3)
Under 15 (%)	29.9	(18.4)	Life expectancy (years, 2010):	52.1	(79.7)
Over 65 (%)	4.8	(14.9)	Males	51.4	(76.9)
			Females	52.8	(82.5)
Latest 5-year average growth (%)	0.8	(0.5)	Last general election:		April 2009

ECONOMY

GDP, current prices (billion USD)	410.7		Value added shares (%):		
GDP, current prices (billion, local currency)	2 964.3		Primary	2.4	(2.6)
Latest 5-year average real growth (%)	2.7	(0.8)	Industry incl. construction	30.6	(27.8)
GDP per capita, PPP (thousand USD)	11.5	(35.4)	Services	67.0	(69.5)

GENERAL GOVERNMENT

Expenditure (% of GDP, 2009)	35.1	(44.9)	Revenue (% of GDP, 2009)	27.4	(36.8)

EXTERNAL ACCOUNTS

Exchange rate (Rand per USD)	7.22		Main exports (% of total merchandise exports, 2010):	
PPP exchange rate (USA = 1)	5.10		Manufactured goods	34.4
Exports of goods and services (% of GDP)	28.8	(52.4)	of which: Non-ferrous metals	16.7
Imports of goods and services (% of GDP)	29.4	(49.3)	Machinery and transport equipment	18.8
Current account balance (% of GDP)	-3.3	(-0.6)	Crude materials, inedible, except fuels	18.3
Net international investment position (% of GDP, 2010)	-17.5		Main imports (% of total merchandise imports, 2010):	
			Machinery and transport equipment	35.4
			Mineral fuels, lubricants and related materials	19.6
			Manufactured goods	10.8
			Chemicals and related products, n.e.s.	10.8

LABOUR MARKET, SKILLS AND INNOVATION

Employment rate (%) for 15-64 year olds:	40.8	(64.9)	Unemployment rate (%):	24.9	(7.9)
Males	47.4	(73)	Youth (%)	49.8	(16.2)
Females	34.6	(56.8)	Long-term unemployed (%)	16.9	(2.6)
Gross domestic expenditure on R&D (% of GDP, 2008)	0.9	(2.4)	Tertiary educational attainment 25-64 year-olds (%, 2007)	4.3	(30.7)

ENVIRONMENT

Total primary energy supply per capita (toe, 2010):	2.7	(4.3)	CO_2 emissions from fuel combustion per capita (tonnes, 2009)	7.4	(9.8)
Renewables (%)	10.7	(8.2)	Water abstractions per capita (m³, 2000)	271.7	
Fine particulate matter concentration (urban, PM10, µg/m³, 2008)	22.1	(22)			

SOCIETY

Income inequality (Gini coefficient, %)	63*	(31.4)	Share of women in parliament (%, July 2012)	41.1	(24.4)
Public and private spending (% of GDP):					
Health care (2009)	8.5	(9.6)			

Note: An average of latest available data is used for the OECD average, calculated when data are available for at least 75% of the member countries.

Source: OECD.STAT (http://stats.oecd.org); OECD Economic Outlook Database.

* Source: World Bank, WDI.

Executive summary

Main findings

South Africa is advancing, but failing to fully achieve its considerable potential. Per capita incomes are growing, public services are expanding, health indicators are improving, crime rates are falling and demographic trends are favourable. The public finances are in better shape than those of many OECD countries, the financial system is healthy and core inflation is stable and within the central bank's target zone. At the same time, an extremely high proportion of the population is out of work, as has been the case for most of the past three decades. Moreover, income inequality remains extremely high, educational outcomes are poor on average and hugely uneven, and frustration is growing with public service delivery failures and corruption. Output growth is sluggish compared to most other middle-income economies. Environmental challenges such as climate change and water scarcity threaten the sustainability of economic growth, while high current account deficits represent a point of macroeconomic vulnerability.

The macroeconomic policy mix has been insufficiently supportive of growth while allowing large budget deficits to persist. The deficit expanded rapidly in cyclically adjusted terms during the crisis and has been brought down only gradually since. Much of the increase in spending came through large increases in the public sector wage bill, while public investment has fallen as a share of total expenditure. With core inflation remaining well contained, monetary policy has been eased cautiously, but not by enough to prevent an increasing degree of slack in the economy. The rand has swung with international sentiment, and has been overvalued for extended periods.

The interaction of weak competition in product markets and dysfunctional labour markets is holding back growth and aggravating unemployment. Most industries are highly concentrated, with network industries dominated by state-owned enterprises, and the weakness of competitive pressures contributes to below-par innovation. Large firms are also able to share the excess returns they make with their employees via collective bargaining, and in many sectors those bargains, including the setting of sectoral minimum wages, are administratively extended to the whole sector, which represents a barrier to entry for small enterprises. The result is a sharply dualised labour market with a well paid formal sector covered by collective bargaining and a secondary market where pay is low and conditions poor. Moreover, millions of South Africans are excluded from work altogether, contributing to poverty, inequality, crime and ill-health. Strengthening product market competition and improving the functioning of labour market institutions should be high priorities, as discussed in the 2010 *Economic Survey of South Africa*.

Education is a critical problem. Skill mismatches represent one aspect of the persistently high unemployment rate, especially for youth: the education system is not producing the skills needed in the labour market. Returns on a high-school certificate, both in terms of finding a job and the earnings premium when employed, are mediocre, while the shortage of skilled workers is reflected in a high premium for university graduates. Shortages of learning materials, teachers, support staff and well-trained principals across most of the school system are among the causes of poor outcomes. If South Africa is to achieve full employment, the quality of basic and vocational education has to be improved.

Greater use of market instruments can help deal with long-term environmental challenges at least cost and with limited demands on scarce administrative capacity. The policy framework for addressing "green" issues, including climate change and water scarcity, is sound, but implementation has so far been slow, in part due to limited administrative capacity. In the electricity and water sectors, there are similar problems: supply is struggling to keep up with demand in a setting in which prices, where they exist, do not cover total costs, let alone reflect environmental externalities. The policy challenge is both to explain the further necessary increases in the relative price of energy and water and bring them about in a manner that minimises adjustment costs and protects the poor.

Key recommendations

Macroeconomic policies

- Adjust the macroeconomic policy mix, using the full available scope to reduce interest rates to support economic activity while reducing the structural budget deficit somewhat faster than currently planned.

- Move towards the introduction of fiscal rules, notably an expenditure rule. Increase the emphasis on the cyclically adjusted balance when setting and explaining fiscal policy.

Labour and product markets

- Curtail the within-sector legal extension of collective bargaining agreements and increase the level of centralisation and co-ordination in collective bargaining to allow for greater influence of outsiders on wages and conditions.

- Make product market regulation less restrictive, particularly as regards barriers to entrepreneurship. Simplify regulations and ease compliance.

Education policy

- Expand the Accelerated Schools Infrastructure Development Initiative programme to address infrastructure backlogs and improve the delivery of learning materials (textbooks, desks, libraries and computers) with priority to the most deprived schools.

- Expand the *Funza Lushaka* bursary programme for teaching studies and allow more immigration of English teachers.

- Provide more school leadership training and support staff in exchange for stricter accountability. Allow the education authorities to appoint and dismiss school principals in a more flexible way (depending on progress on school performance in Annual National Assessments and on external reviews), while making school principals responsible for yearly teacher evaluations and monitoring teachers' daily attendance.

- Empower the independent federal evaluation unit NEEDU, join the Programme for International Student Assessment (PISA) and the Teaching and Learning International Survey (TALIS) and undertake an OECD *Review of Evaluation and Assessment Frameworks for Improving School Outcomes*.

- Foster on-the-job training with tax credits and simplify administrative procedures for hiring trainees from FET colleges. Widen the scope for apprenticeship programmes organised by public-private partnerships.

Policies to achieve greener growth

- In designing climate change mitigation policies, favour broad and easy-to-implement instruments with limited demands on administrative capacity, such as a simple carbon tax.

- Reduce implicit and explicit subsidies for energy and coal consumption, and use other instruments, such as cash transfers or supply vouchers, for protecting the poor.

- Accelerate the allocation of water-use licenses and ensure that charges for water reflect supply costs and scarcity.

Assessment and recommendations

Overcoming entrenched problems will require stepped-up policy efforts

Despite considerable success on many economic and social policy fronts over the past 19 years, South Africa faces a number of long-standing economic problems that still reflect at least in part the long-lasting and harmful legacy of apartheid. One is a lack of economic dynamism: convergence towards advanced country per capita income levels has been slower than in most other emerging economies (Figure 1A). The fastest-growing countries tend to have low per capita income, but even taking into account starting levels South Africa's growth has been relatively slow (Figure 1B). Above all, employment remains too low and unemployment excessively high, which exacerbates a range of social problems and tensions. One aspect of this central problem is that educational outcomes are poor on average and extremely uneven, which aggravates the excess supply of unskilled labour as well as worsening income inequality. In addition, the prospects for sustained improvements in well-being are compromised by environmental challenges, notably climate change and water stress. As well articulated in the National Development Plan (NDP) published in August 2012, South Africa needs to achieve rapid, inclusive economic growth while at the same time making the transition to a low-carbon economy and managing effectively the country's scarce water resources. Tackling the key problems effectively will require continued skilful management of macroeconomic policies, as part of the process of providing helpful framework conditions for economic activity, but above all improved implementation of structural policies, with education being a particularly critical area.

Growth has been sluggish since the crisis, and is expected to pick up only gradually

South Africa has so far experienced a relatively weak recovery from the 2008-09 recession, with post-crisis growth performance more similar to the OECD average than the more dynamic BRIIC group (Figure 2A). Estimating potential growth rates is always an imprecise exercise, and all the more so for a country with such a high rate of inactivity and where the responsiveness of wage and price inflation to changes in unemployment is low. In addition, in recent years the task has been further complicated by uncertainty over the extent to which electricity supply limitations have constrained potential output growth in South Africa. That said, real GDP growth has been below estimated potential every year from 2008 through 2012 (except for 2011, when the two were roughly in line), implying a growing degree of slack in the economy: OECD estimates put the negative output gap at close to 3% currently (Figure 3). While some other estimates are lower, most observers agree that the gap is significantly negative and likely to have widened in 2012 and to do so again in 2013 (Table 1).

The statistical data for Israel are supplied by and under the responsibility of the relevant Israeli authorities. The use of such data by the OECD is without prejudice to the status of the Golan Heights, East Jerusalem and Israeli settlements in the West Bank under the terms of international law.

Figure 1. **Per capita income growth has been slower than in most other major emerging economies**

A. The rate of catch-up in income levels has been gradual

Level of GDP per capita (constant 2005 PPPs), relative to OECD

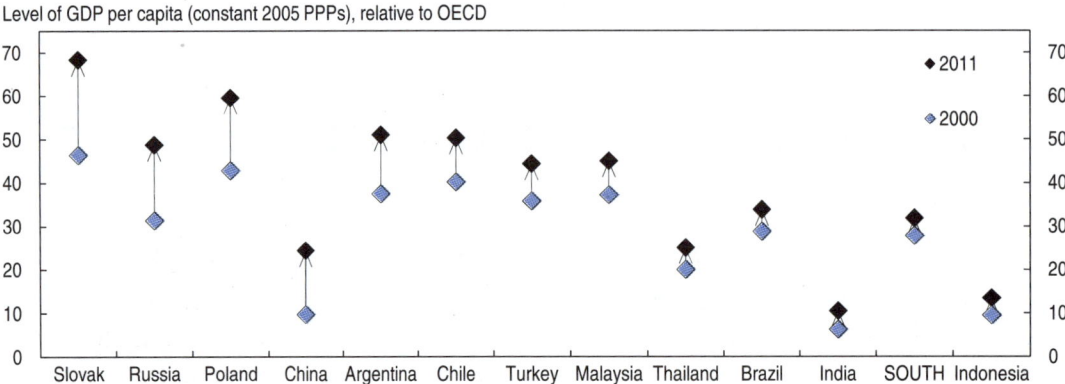

B. Growth has been relatively slow even adjusting for initial income levels

GDP per capita (constant 2005 PPPs), annual percentage change, 2000-11

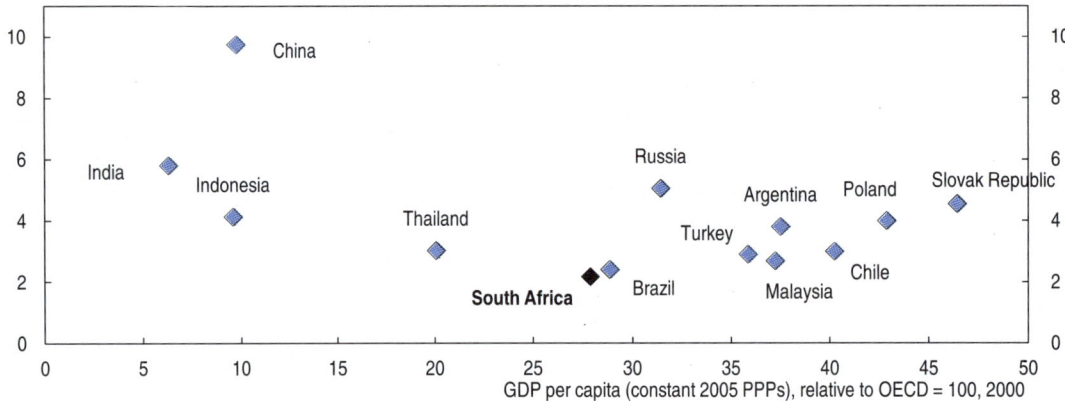

Source: World Bank, *World Development Indicators online Database.*

Note for Panel A: The light-coloured diamond shows the income level in 2000 as a percentage of the level in the OECD. The darker diamond shows this level in 2011, with the arrow indicating the change between 2000 and 2011.

Note for Panel B: The vertical axis shows the average annual growth rate of GDP per capita between 2000 and 2011, while the horizontal axis measures the level of income per capita in 2000 as a percentage of the OECD. It is usually expected that countries with a lower initial income level will growth faster than those with higher initial income levels.

StatLink ⟶ http://dx.doi.org/10.1787/888932782717

Such a long period of increasing output gaps is unusual, raising the question of whether potential growth rates were actually lower than estimated. If so, then the extent of idle resources would be correspondingly less. However, South Africa is also affected by the slow recovery from the international financial crisis, which is further aggravated by the slow resolution of euro area deficiencies. Estimates of potential growth have indeed been reduced in recent years, since low investment activity slows down capital deepening while the persistence of high rates of long-term unemployment and discouraged labour force participation erodes human capital, thereby raising the structural inactivity rate. Nonetheless, there is considerable evidence of slack in the economy. Notably, although the working-age population has been growing by some 1½ per cent a year, employment is still

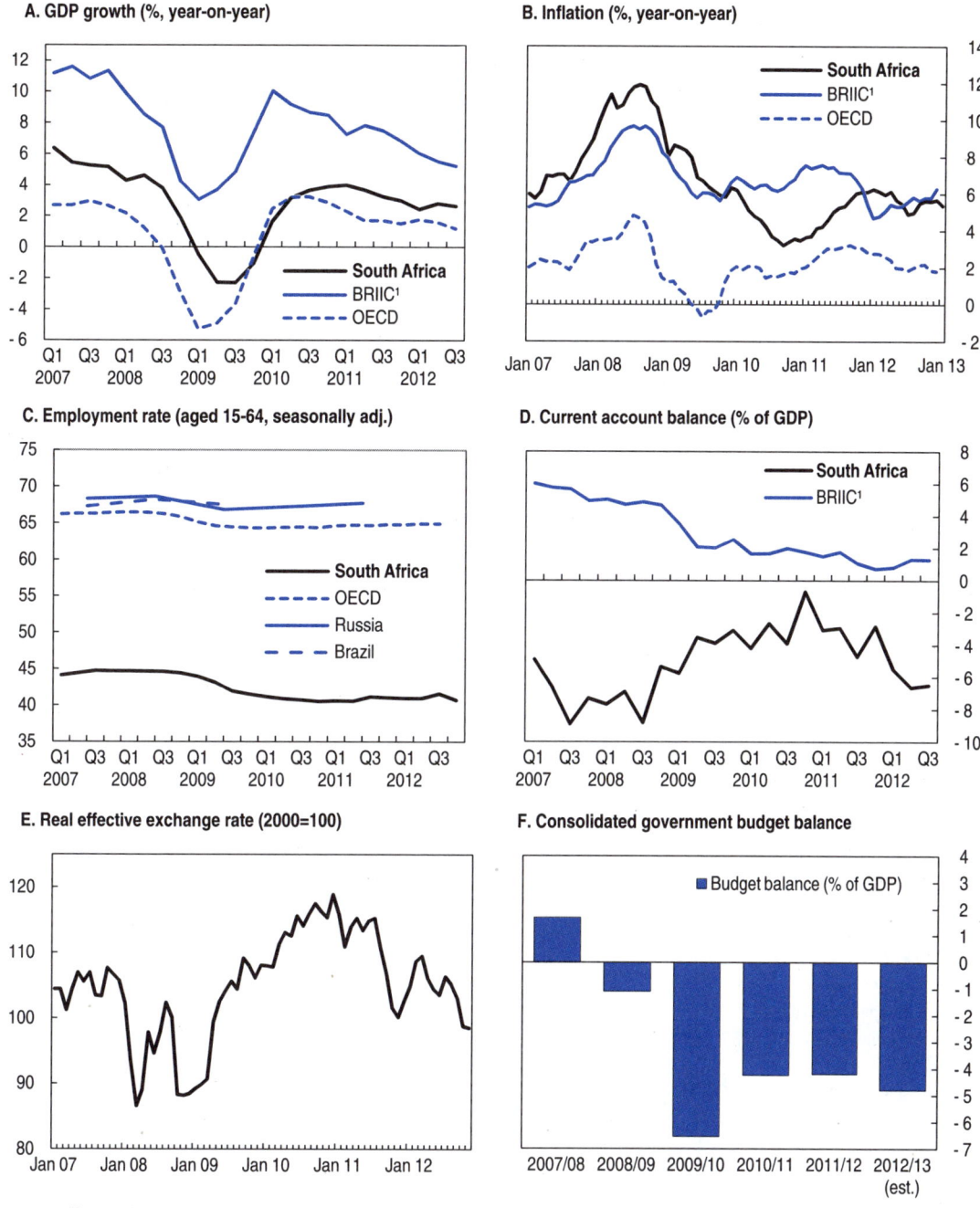

Figure 2. **Selected economic indicators**

1. Brazil, Russian Federation, India, Indonesia and China. Simple, unweighted average for inflation.
Source: OECD Quarterly National Accounts Database; OECD Monthly Economic Indicators Database; OECD Short-Term Labour Market Statistics Database; Statistics South Africa; South Africa Reserve Bank Database; National Treasury; OECD Economic Outlook 92 Database.

StatLink ᘐᘵᔈ *http://dx.doi.org/10.1787/888932782736*

3% lower than in late 2008, and the broad measure of unemployment, including discouraged job-seekers, was at 33.4% in the third quarter of 2012, up nearly 7 percentage points from the fourth quarter of 2008. Also, despite a rebound since 2010, manufacturing output, electricity production and capacity utilisation remain well below pre-crisis peaks, as does mining output and real credit to the private sector (Figure 4).

Figure 3. **The negative output gap is still widening**

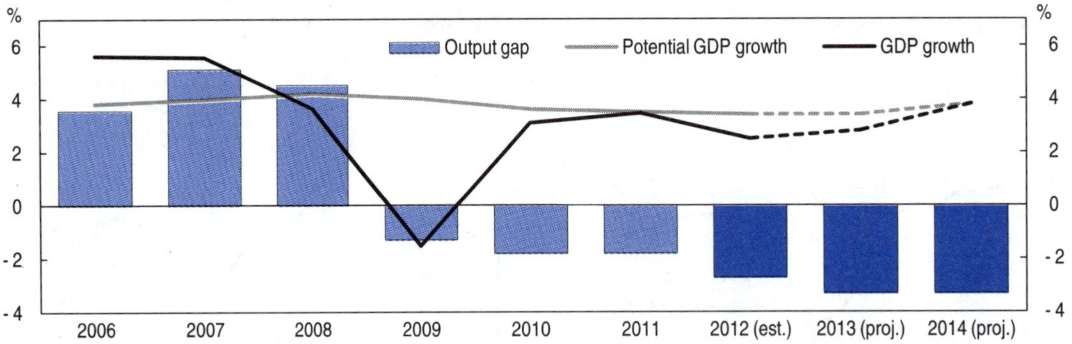

Source: OECD estimates.

How to read this figure: The output gap (the bars) measures the difference between actual and potential real GDP as a percentage of potential GDP. It is negative when the level of actual real GDP is below the level of potential. The lines show the growth of actual and potential real GDP. When actual growth is below potential growth, the output gap is becoming more negative or less positive.

StatLink ᵃᵐˢ⯑ http://dx.doi.org/10.1787/888932782755

Table 1. **Selected economic indicators**

	2009	2010	2011	2012	2013	2014
	Percentage changes, volume (2005 prices)					
GDP	-1.5	3.1	3.5	2.5	2.8	3.8
Private consumption	-1.6	4.4	4.8	3.0	2.9	4.0
Government consumption	4.8	5.0	4.6	3.6	3.3	3.5
Gross fixed capital formation	-4.3	-2.0	4.5	6.5	4.5	6.6
Final domestic demand	-0.8	3.1	4.7	3.4	3.3	4.5
Stockbuilding[1]	-1.0	1.3	0.3	0.1	0.0	0.0
Total domestic demand	-1.6	4.4	4.6	3.4	3.3	4.4
Exports of goods and services	-19.5	4.5	5.9	0.7	3.7	7.0
Imports of goods and services	-17.4	9.6	9.7	5.9	3.6	7.6
Net exports[1]	-0.2	-1.5	-1.1	-1.1	-0.3	-0.8
Memorandum items						
GDP deflator	8.3	7.2	6.0	5.5	5.0	4.8
Consumer price index	7.1	4.3	5.0	5.6	5.4	5.0
Private consumption deflator	6.5	3.9	5.0	5.6	5.3	4.9
Unemployment rate	23.9	24.9	24.9	25.1	24.3	23.8
Output gap	-1.3	-1.8	-1.8	-2.7	-3.3	-3.3
Household saving ratio[2]	-0.7	-0.3	-0.1	0.0	0.1	0.0
General government financial balance[3]	-4.9	-6.0	-5.3	-5.0	-4.7	-4.0
National government gross debt[3]	30.9	35.3	39.2	40.0	41.0	41.3
Current account balance[3]	-4.0	-2.8	-3.4	-6.0	-6.1	-6.2

Note: National accounts are based on official chain-linked data. This introduces a discrepancy in the identity between real demand components and GDP. For further details see OECD Economic Outlook Sources and Methods (www.oecd.org/eco/sources-and-methods).
1. Contributions to changes in real GDP (percentage of real GDP in previous years).
2. As a percentage of disposable income.
3. As a percentage of GDP.
Source: Statistics South Africa and OECD estimates.

The reason for the long period of actual growth lagging behind potential is that the economy has faced a number of headwinds. For example, after an initial fast rebound, private consumption growth slowed, reflecting in part the heavy initial burden of household debt, which reduced households' ability and willingness to finance

Figure 4. **Several economic indicators are still below pre-crisis peaks**

Latest 3-month period compared to pre-2009 peak level, seasonally adjusted, %

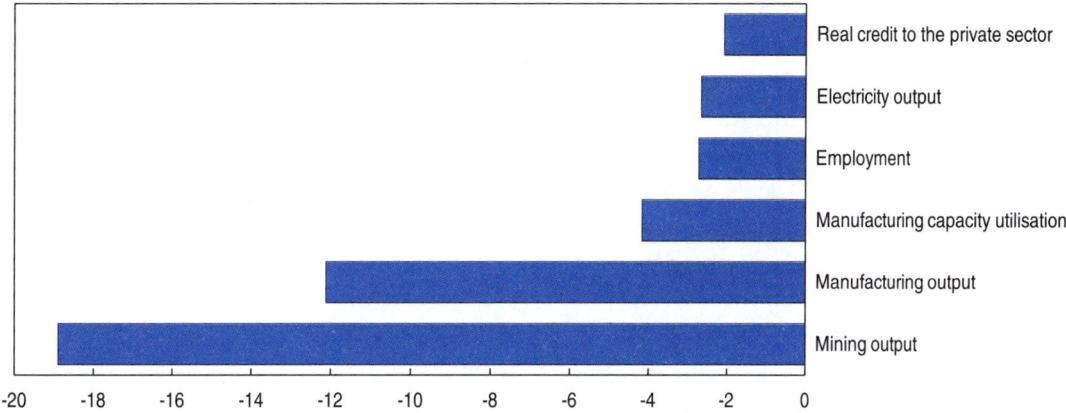

Source: OECD calculations based on Statistics South Africa and South Africa Reserve Bank Database.

StatLink ᴍᴤᴾ http://dx.doi.org/10.1787/888932782774

consumption with new loans. On the contrary, they started to repair their balance sheets-household debt fell relative to disposable income from its pre-crisis peak in early 2008 through late 2011 before stabilising (Figure 5A). The propensity to consume was also undermined by falling house prices and, for some of the period, equity prices; despite having recovered from the low-point at end-2008, household net wealth was still slightly lower in real terms at end-2011 than in 2006 (Figure 5B).

Figure 5. **Households have struggled to reduce debt loads and rebuild net wealth**

A. Household debt to disposible income of households, %, seasonally adjusted

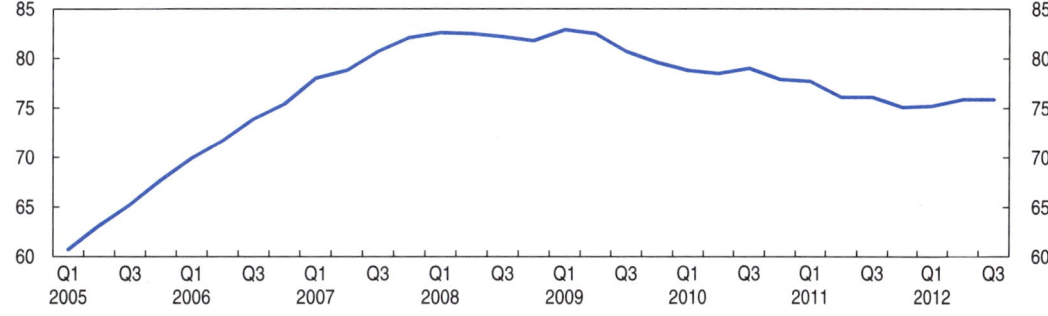

B. Real household net wealth (deflated by CPI, index 2005 = 100)

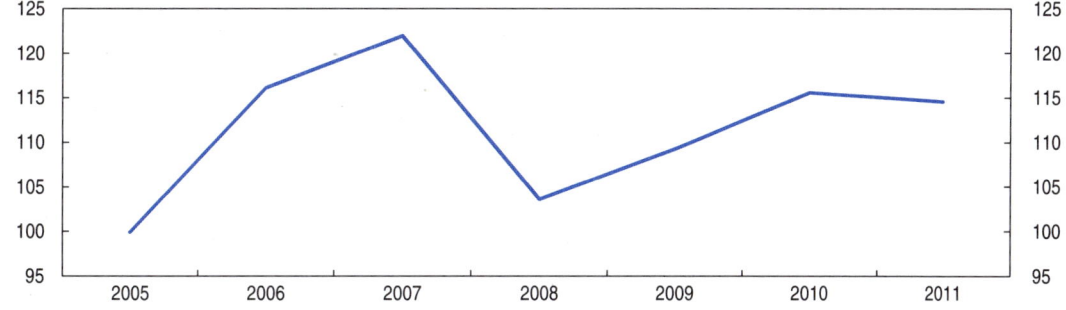

Source: OECD calculations based on South Africa Reserve Bank Database and Statistics South Africa.

StatLink ᴍᴤᴾ http://dx.doi.org/10.1787/888932782793

Another headwind has been the sub-par post-crisis recovery of the global economy. The increase in OECD output in the 4 years since the crisis has been smaller than in other post-recession recoveries in recent decades, even though the recent recession was unusually deep (Figure 6). Moreover, the global outlook deteriorated over the last two years and remains fragile. Indicators of business sentiment and orders have worsened recently in both major OECD and non-OECD economies, with the euro zone being an area of particular weakness. The subdued global recovery has both implied relatively slow growth of markets for South Africa's exports and depressed confidence. The latter effect probably explains part of the anomalous weakness of private fixed investment. Despite record-low domestic interest rates, and notwithstanding an uninterrupted increase in corporate gross operating surpluses (even through the crisis), gross private fixed capital formation remains below pre-crisis levels (Figure 7). Moreover, much of the recovery in non-government investment since 2009 has been accounted for by state-owned enterprises undertaking major infrastructure-building programmes. The reticence of the private sector to borrow or spend out of growing cash balances is almost certainly linked to gloom about economic prospects, reinforced by domestic political uncertainty and outbreaks of social instability.

Figure 6. **The recovery from the latest recession in OECD economies has been unusually weak**

Total domestic demand index (1 at time t)

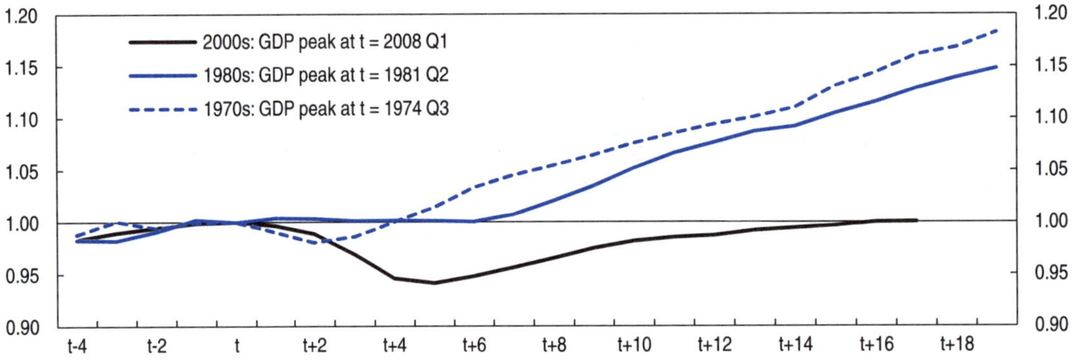

- 2000s: GDP peak at t = 2008 Q1
- 1980s: GDP peak at t = 1981 Q2
- 1970s: GDP peak at t = 1974 Q3

Source: OECD Economic Outlook 92 Database.

StatLink http://dx.doi.org/10.1787/888932782812

Figure 7. **Private investment has decoupled from corporate profits**

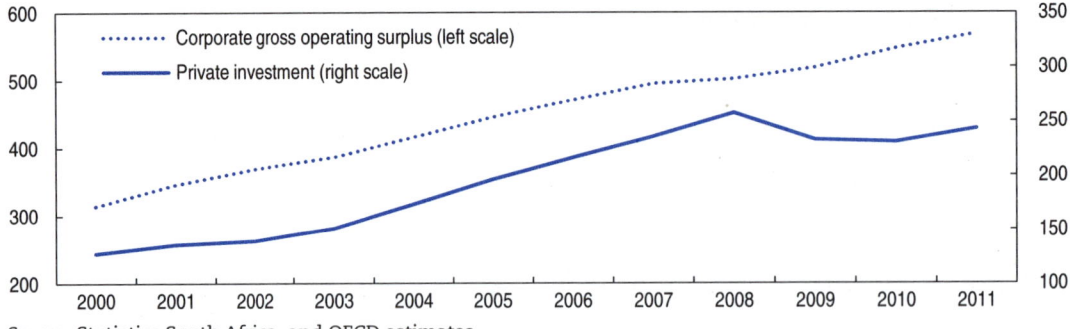

- Corporate gross operating surplus (left scale)
- Private investment (right scale)

Source: Statistics South Africa, and OECD estimates.

StatLink http://dx.doi.org/10.1787/888932782831

The overvaluation of the rand was another drag on output growth since the crisis. The 35% rise of the real effective exchange rate over the two years through late 2010 was one reason why import demand grew much more rapidly than export volumes from late 2009 on, resulting in negative contributions of net exports to real GDP growth of 1.5 and 1.1 percentage points in 2010 and 2011 respectively. The pressures for appreciation of the rand were largely associated with waves of portfolio inflows during "risk-on" episodes in international capital markets (driven in part by monetary easing in the United States and Europe). The shifts in appetites for emerging market financial assets accentuate the volatility of South Africa's exchange rate, which is anyway high given the variability of the prices of its export commodities. This volatility has costs via heightened uncertainty about the profitability of investment in the tradables sector, but such costs are of second order compared to those associated with prolonged overvaluation.

The rand has depreciated by about 17% in real effective terms since December 2010, mostly as a result of weaker risk appetites in the context of the worsening euro area crisis and a more general global slowdown, reinforced more recently by the mining strikes and political uncertainty. This has unwound some of the earlier appreciation. Nonetheless, the recent IMF Article IV staff report estimated that as of March 2012 the rand was still overvalued by between 5 and 15%, with the External Sustainability approach suggesting misalignment of over 20%, and the currency has depreciated by only about 10% in real terms since then. Thus, while the issue of overvaluation has diminished of late, it could quickly re-emerge in the event of a renewed upturn in sentiment towards emerging markets, especially if combined with an easing of industrial relations tensions. The likely persistence of very low interest rates in major advanced economies for some time to come means that the probability of further waves of liquidity flows towards emerging markets is high.

A more recent negative growth factor is the weakening of key export prices. The uptrend in the terms of trade from 2000 to 2011 helped mask the weakness of export volumes and contributed to a. narrowing of the current account deficit during and immediately after the recession. From mid-2011, however, the prices of several major export commodities reversed course (Figure 8). The slowdown in China, whose rapid growth had driven much of the increase in demand for metals and fuels in the 2000s, was a key swing factor. The downturn in commodity prices, particularly when combined with the rash of wildcat mining strikes that affected the mining sector in the third and fourth quarters of 2012, is likely to be reflected in weaker near-term investment and consumption than otherwise. While OECD projections foresee recovering growth in China and broadly stable commodity prices in 2013-14, a further fall in major commodity export prices is a downside risk for the South African economy.

One positive feature in the performance of the economy through the crisis and beyond has been the robustness of the financial system. For a middle income country, South Africa has an unusually developed and well supervised financial system, and the banking system came through the 2008-09 recession in relatively good health. The major banks enjoy comfortable levels of capital adequacy, returns on equity and assets remained positive through the crisis and have recovered steadily since and nonperforming loans have been declining since mid-2009 (Figure 9). Lending growth has been slower to recover, reflecting weak demand in a context of falling house prices and sluggish economic growth as well as tightening lending standards. At the same time, unsecured lending to households has been increasing rapidly of late, raising some concerns about excessive borrowing, although the

Figure 8. **Export commodity prices have turned down recently**

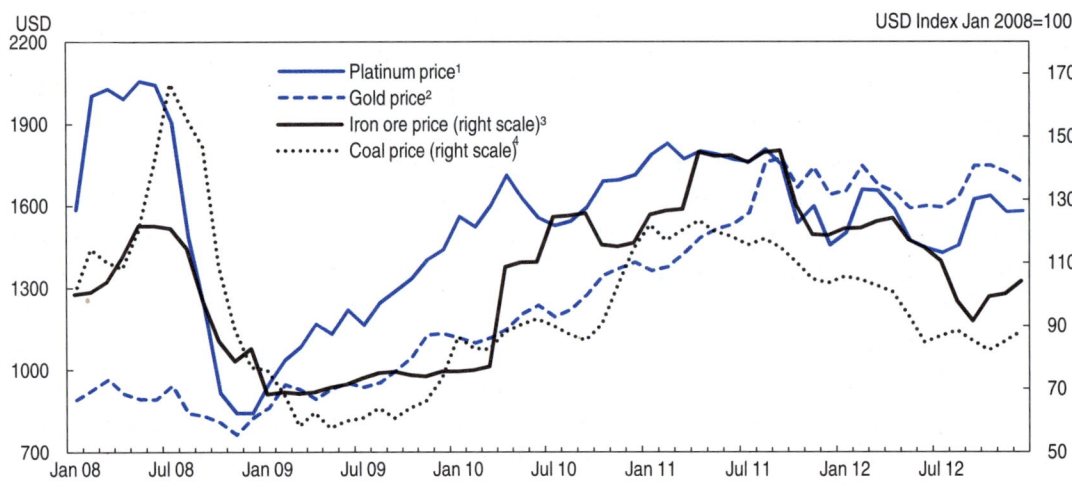

1. London Platinum Free Market USD/Troy oz.
2. Gold Bullion London Bullion Market USD/Troy Ounce.
3. Hamburg Institute for Economic Research, world market price, iron ore, scrap.
4. South African Thermal, USD per metric tonne.
Source: IMF, *IFS Database on line*, Datastream and HWWA.

StatLink ᵐᵗˢ⁵ *http://dx.doi.org/10.1787/888932782850*

level of such lending remains small relative to total bank assets and therefore not a systemic risk.

The macroeconomic policy mix should support growth while strengthening public finances

Given the slack in the economy and the subdued prospects for near-term growth, the macroeconomic policy mix should aim to boost domestic demand. This would be best accomplished via a combination of tighter fiscal policy and monetary easing, as this would deliver policy stimulus while avoiding upward pressure on the exchange rate, supporting national saving and safeguarding fiscal sustainability.

Fiscal policy tightening should be more ambitious, but with full play for automatic stabilisers

Prudent management of the public finances going back to the 1990s created room for counter-cyclical fiscal policy when the global crisis struck in 2008. The deficit was allowed to expand sharply at that time, cushioning the blow to domestic demand. Even so, the public debt burden remains moderate and domestic and external borrowing costs for the government are at or near record low levels, notwithstanding recent downgrades by international rating agencies. Nonetheless, in cyclically adjusted terms the budget has been in deficit for the whole of the last economic cycle. The cyclically adjusted deficit was significantly reduced in 2010/11, but has been little changed since (Figure 10).

The government's current medium-term budget plan implies continued gradual reduction of the cyclically adjusted deficit, which would see the debt-to-GDP ratio begin to decline in 2015/16 (Figure 11). While fiscal sustainability is therefore not under immediate threat, it would be unwise to take risks by allowing large cyclically adjusted deficits to persist for many years. The current medium-term budget plan implies a reduction in the cyclically adjusted deficit of about 1½ percentage points of GDP between 2011/12 and 2015/16

Figure 9. **The banks are profitable and well capitalised, with falling levels of bad loans**

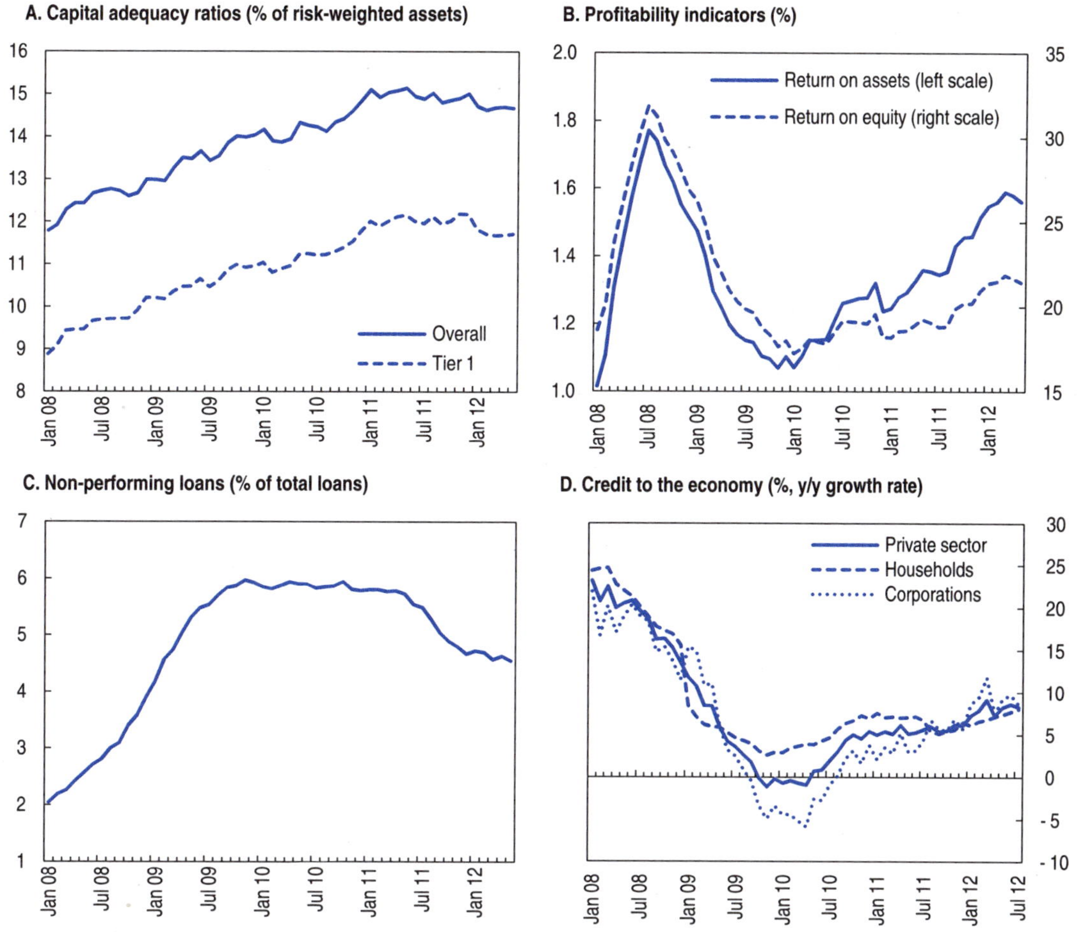

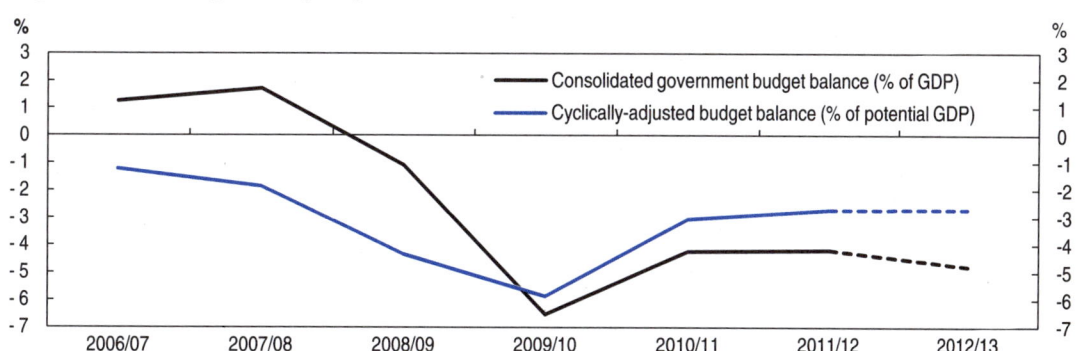

A. Capital adequacy ratios (% of risk-weighted assets)

B. Profitability indicators (%)

C. Non-performing loans (% of total loans)

D. Credit to the economy (%, y/y growth rate)

Source: IMF Financial Soundness Indicators Database and South African Reserve Bank Database.

StatLink ⟮ms⟯ http://dx.doi.org/10.1787/888932782869

Figure 10. **The cyclically adjusted deficit widened in the crisis and remains sizable**

Note: The cyclically adjusted budget balance is above (below) the actual balance when real GDP is below (above) potential, that is, when the output gap is negative (positive).

Source: National Treasury and OECD estimates.

StatLink ⟮ms⟯ http://dx.doi.org/10.1787/888932782888

Figure 11. **Public debt is projected to stabilise at moderate levels**

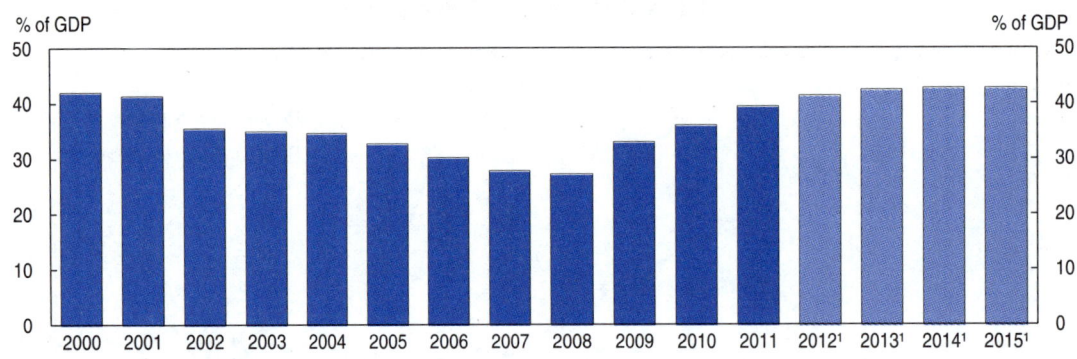

Note: Gross debt of the central government, excluding extra-budgetary institutions and social security funds. Fiscal years (1 April-31 March).
1. As projected at the end of October 2012.
Source: National Treasury, 2012 Budget Review and Medium Term Budget Policy Statement, 2012.

StatLink ⬛ᴵˢᴾ http://dx.doi.org/10.1787/888932782907

according to OECD estimates, which would leave the cyclically adjusted deficit at 1.3% of GDP in 2015/16. While, in the short term, revenue slippages due to slower-than-expected growth can be accommodated by allowing higher deficits than originally planned, given the fragility of growth, the consolidation of the cyclically adjusted deficit should if anything be speeded up. A reasonable goal would be to bring the cyclically adjusted balance below 1% of GDP in 2015/16. This modest additional fiscal tightening would help to contain the widening of the current account deficit and ease pressures for overvaluation of the rand by putting further downward pressure on interest rates.

Fiscal consolidation should be accompanied by a shift to investment, which would support the government's efforts to eliminate key infrastructure backlogs. Since the onset of the global crisis in 2008, the growth of government investment has slowed while current spending and especially the wage bill have expanded rapidly. This compositional shift was unfortunate given the existence of pressing infrastructure shortages, the need for the expansion of the cyclically adjusted deficit to be undone fairly quickly to safeguard fiscal sustainability and the effect of large public sector wage increases on collective bargaining outcomes in the private sector. The planned reorientation of public expenditure from current to capital spending over the medium term, as outlined in the 2013 Medium Term Expenditure Framework Guidelines, is therefore well judged. Public sector wage moderation is likely to be a key part of this shift, since the rebalancing of spending should be accomplished while deficits are being brought down.

Apart from restraining current expenditure, the government will probably have to use revenue measures to reduce the cyclically adjusted deficit over the medium term while at the same time funding infrastructure needs and increased spending in other high-priority areas, like education. Selected measures to raise additional revenue can go hand in hand with initiatives to address negative externalities, such as taxing environmentally harmful activities. More generally, if revenues are increased while reorienting the tax mix toward more growth-friendly taxation, by reducing taxation of corporate profits (not including resource rents) and raising property taxes, the negative effects on growth could be minimised.

Although the National Treasury has proved highly competent at managing the public finances, neither its concentration of technical expertise nor its consistent advocacy for fiscal prudence have turned out to be sufficient to prevent spending from rising rapidly in good years. As discussed in Chapter 2 of the 2010 *Economic Survey of South Africa*, an evolution of the fiscal policy framework could help reduce the likelihood of procyclical policies in both booms and busts. One measure proposed at that time was a rule capping expenditure, in order to better resist pressures for more spending when revenues are cyclically strong. The government has taken a step in that direction, with the 2013 Medium Term Expenditure Framework Guidelines ruling out any increase in spending in 2013/14 and 2014/15 relative to the projections in the 2012 Budget. The 2010 *Survey* also recommended that the Treasury continue to refine its estimation of the cyclically adjusted balance and put increasing emphasis on it in its analysis and objective-setting. While there has been no clear trend towards using the concept of the cyclically adjusted balance in discussing objectives, the government has reiterated its intention to reduce the structural deficit and create the fiscal space to respond to future variations in the business cycle and external shocks. In that context, the National Treasury is preparing a long-term fiscal report, expected to be issued in 2013, that assesses the sustainability of spending options in light of demographic and economic projections.

There appears to be room for a further easing of monetary policy

As discussed above, the sluggishness of the recovery to date is largely attributable to unfavourable exogenous factors: weak demand for exports, surges in capital inflows that worsened rand overvaluation, high initial household debt burdens and international crises that negatively affected expectations about growth. Not all these factors were fully foreseen beforehand. Thus the South African Reserve Bank (SARB), along with most others, did not predict the extent to which the output gap in South Africa would remain wide, and thus overestimated underlying inflationary pressures. Gauging the balance of risks was difficult, particularly when, as from late 2010 to late 2011, world food and energy prices were rising strongly, driving up headline inflation (Figure 12A).

Figure 12. **Inflation has fluctuated with food and fuel prices, but core inflation has been stable**

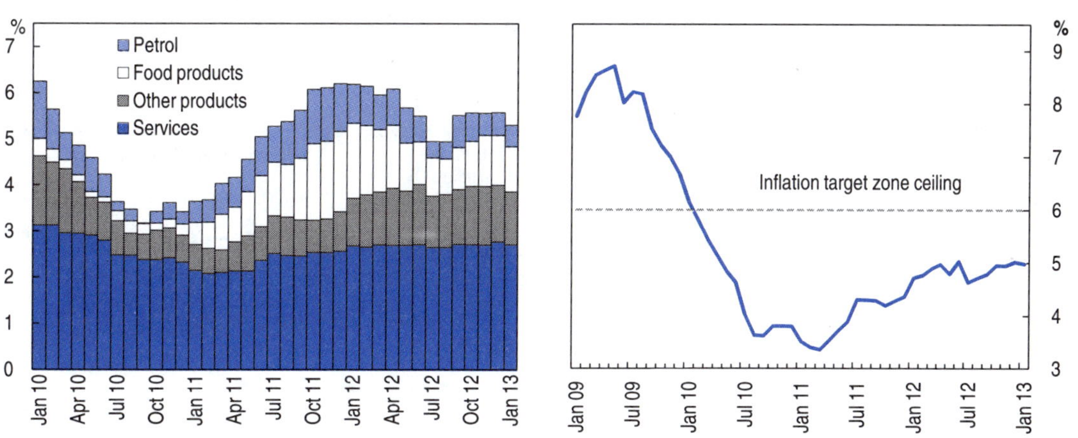

1. CPI excluding food and non-alcoholic beverages and petrol.
Source: OECD estimates based on Statistics South Africa.

StatLink ⬛⬛ *http://dx.doi.org/10.1787/888932782926*

Renewed food price increases associated with unfavourable weather in various key growing areas have exerted renewed upward pressure on headline inflation, but core inflation has remained well within the SARB's inflation target range (Figure 12B), while growth and employment risks continue to appear skewed to the downside. The annual growth of unit labour costs has been falling, and has been negative in real terms since early 2011, implying that unit labour costs are exerting downward pressure on producer price inflation (Figure 13A). Collective bargaining settlements in the private sector have also been on a downtrend since 2008 (Figure 13B), suggesting that economy-wide wage pressures are easing, notwithstanding the recent high-profile mining disputes. Meanwhile, compared to other economies with sizable negative output gaps, South Africa has higher real interest rates (Figure 14). Taken together, this suggests that there remains scope for some further easing of monetary policy.

Figure 13. **Wage push pressures have been easing**

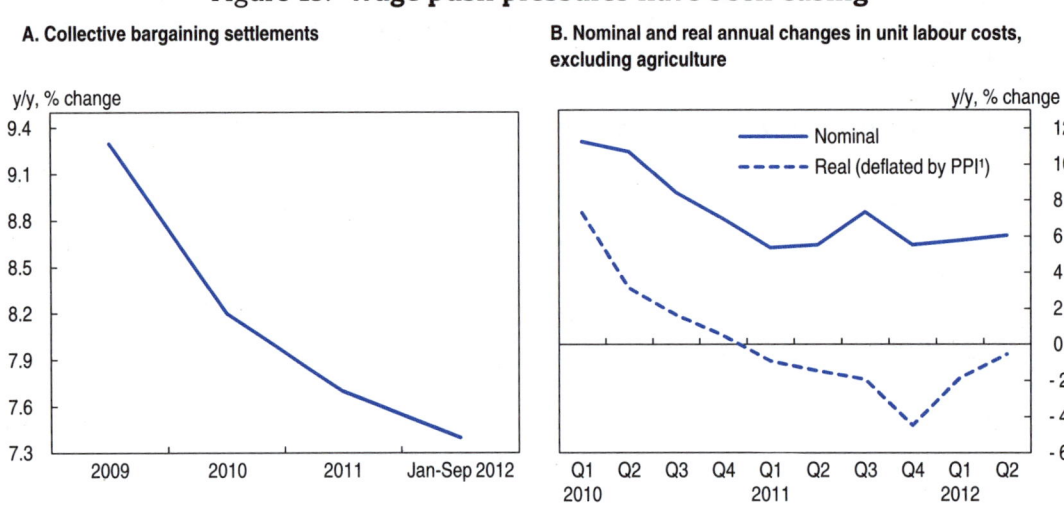

A. Collective bargaining settlements

B. Nominal and real annual changes in unit labour costs, excluding agriculture

1. Producer price index.
Source: South Africa Reserve Bank and Andrew Levy, *Wage Settlement Survey* quarterly reports.

StatLink ⟪ http://dx.doi.org/10.1787/888932782945

Figure 14. **Real short-term interest rates are low in absolute but not relative terms**

Money market rate deflated by consumer price inflation (4 quarter forward)

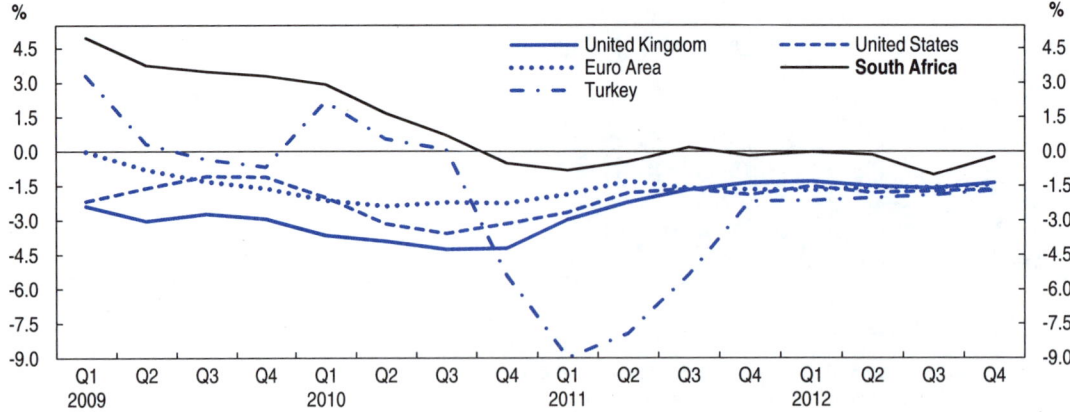

Source: OECD calculations based on OECD, *Economics Department's Analytical Database* and IMF, *IFS Database*.

StatLink ⟪ http://dx.doi.org/10.1787/888932782964

One concern about a possible easing is that lower interest rates would cause a sharp weakening of the rand, which in turn would bring little if any competitive gains for the tradables sector because the passthrough to wages and prices would be close to 100%, preventing a change in the real exchange rate. Past experience gives little support for such fears: there were three episodes of substantial nominal depreciation (ranging from 20 to 42%) since 2000, and on average the real effective exchange rate moved by about three quarters of the amount of the nominal effective rate.

A related challenge for the SARB is to play a role in avoiding overvaluation of the currency, which is also a factor behind slow growth (Prasad *et al.*, 2007), rising external imbalances and an excessive accumulation of foreign currency-denominated debt. This pattern is broadly consistent with South Africa's experience in recent years, with a surge in inflows in 2010 being associated with a large increase in the real effective exchange rate, a deterioration of export performance and a reversal in the narrowing of current account deficits – the current account deficit widened from 3.5% of GDP in the third quarter of 2009 to 4.1% in the same quarter of 2011, despite a 12% improvement in the terms of trade over the same period. Moreover, swings in capital flows often appear to reflect mainly shifts in sentiment towards emerging markets and/or commodity prices rather than South-Africa-specific fundamentals: the movements of South Africa's exchange rate usually mirror closely those of emerging market exchange rates in general (Figure 15). South Africa and other emerging markets with floating exchange rates are sometimes "innocent bystanders", affected by actions such as quantitative easing in advanced countries and the policy of quasi-fixed exchange rates with enormous reserve accumulation by other emerging economies.

Figure 15. **The exchange rate tends to move in step with those of other emerging market currencies**

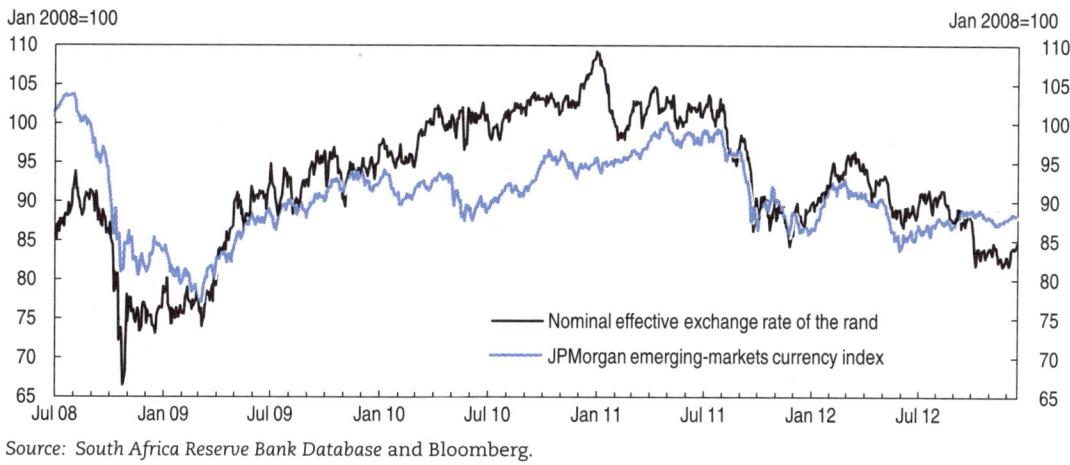

Source: *South Africa Reserve Bank Database* and Bloomberg.

StatLink ᴍᴤᴘ *http://dx.doi.org/10.1787/888932782983*

This underlines the case for being prepared to meet any renewed strong pressures for rand appreciation with a range of responses, beginning with a shift in the macroeconomic policy mix, *i.e.* a tightening of fiscal policy combined with a reduction of interest rates, within the constraints imposed by the inflation-targeting framework. As noted by the recent IMF policy paper on the management of capital flows (IMF, 2012) other supporting measures can also be envisaged, depending on country-specific circumstances. In South

Africa's case, where reserves are no more than adequate and there is probably already a degree of overvaluation, such measures could include more active foreign exchange market intervention, increased efforts to communicate official views on the equilibrium level of the exchange rate, further liberalisation of capital outflows and, if necessary, the introduction of temporary market-based disincentives for destabilising short-term capital inflows. None of these methods alone is certain to be effective, and they generally have costs as well as expected benefits. Nonetheless, the economic damage from prolonged overvaluation probably warrants a more comprehensive response than seen to date as and when pressures for appreciation intensify again. On a more long-term basis, structural policies that facilitate a reduction in domestic costs can also be useful in avoiding upward drift of the real exchange rate. Although adjustments to macroeconomic policies can help to reduce the degree of slack in the economy while also containing external imbalances, South Africa's main economic problems are primarily structural in nature, and structural policy deficiencies in several areas need to be addressed if these problems are to be resolved.

Box 1. **Main macroeconomic policy recommendations**

- Adjust the macroeconomic policy mix, using the full available scope to reduce interest rates to support economic activity while reducing the structural budget deficit somewhat faster than currently planned.
- In the short term, given the fragility of growth, accommodate revenue slippages from slower-than-expected growth via higher deficits.
- Reorient public expenditure from current to capital spending, to address infrastructure shortages.
- Move towards the introduction of fiscal rules, notably an expenditure rule. Increase the emphasis on the cyclically adjusted balance when setting and explaining fiscal policy.
- Explore means to resist renewed pressures for overvaluation of the rand, including more active intervention, increased efforts to communicate official views on whether the exchange rate is deviating significantly from an equilibrium level, further liberalisation of capital outflows and, if necessary, the introduction of temporary market-based disincentives for short-term capital inflows.

Unfulfilled hopes for improved economic conditions for the majority are fuelling frustration

Since the end of apartheid, South Africa has made progress towards establishing a more equitable society, but there have also been failings. Prominent among these is the inability to reduce income inequality. South Africa's Gini coefficient, at around 0.70, is among the highest in the world. Income differences appear to be even starker within South Africa than at the global level, as the world income inequality Gini, pooling all incomes across all countries, was estimated at 0.62 in 2008 (Morrisson and Murtin, 2012). In comparison, the Gini index was equal to 54.7 in Brazil and 40.1 in the Russian Federation in 2009. Although advances in areas such as electrification and access to education have increased equality of opportunities (World Bank, 2012a), no progress towards income equality has been made since the end of apartheid. In the 2010 *Income and Expenditure Survey* the income ratio between the top and bottom deciles was around 20, far above the level of 5 in the United States, one of the most unequal countries in the OECD (OECD, 2012a).

As a consequence of South Africa's legacy of discrimination, ethnicity accounts for a large part of income inequality. The within-race inequality component is also substantial, however, and has increased tremendously. The Gini coefficient for Africans has increased from 0.55 to 0.62 between 1993 and 2008, and from 0.42 to 0.50 for Whites.

Inequality is also tightly bound up with labour market outcomes. As shown by Leibbrandt et al. (2010), labour market income contributed 85% of income inequality in 2008. Much of that is driven by the large number of individuals with no labour income, given the high incidence of unemployment and inactivity. However, inequality among households with labour market earnings is also high, as real earnings in the bottom deciles have not risen in the post-apartheid period and have fallen markedly relative to earnings in the top deciles.

Apart from equity considerations, reducing inequality may have a positive economic pay-off per se, as negative externalities, such as crime, appear to be causally linked to inequality in South Africa (Demombynes and Özler, 2005). The government has used the tax and benefit system to alleviate inequality, and these efforts have had some impact. Leibbrandt et al. (2010) estimate that redistributive policies have undone about 40% of the increase in the market-income inequality (measured by the Gini coefficient), with the expansion of social transfers being particularly important. Even so, many South Africans of working age have no labour earnings, no income on assets and no unemployment benefits or other transfers, and survive only with support from their family. Despite an increase in the progressivity of taxes since 1993 and the expansion of social transfers, the reduction of inequality attributable to taxes and transfers remains well below OECD levels.

Limited administrative capacity, especially at the sub-national government level, is one of the constraints to building a more inclusive society. While provincial administrations have received adequate budgets to solve specific problems (e.g. the supply of textbooks to schools), little change has occurred on the ground in some provinces. Given limited capacity, it is generally advisable to formulate more modest development plans and focus on implementation and outcomes. The former housing policy (going back to the Reconstruction and Development Programme of 1994) is an example of an overly ambitious plan that failed to eliminate precarious settlements and the housing deficit affecting 2.1 million households by 2010. Thanks to a proper assessment of this failure and a shift in approach, a new National Upgrading Support Programme was established in 2010 with the objective of endowing informal settlements with basic infrastructure, including schools, in an incremental way.

Even when state intervention is put in place effectively, informational problems arise, especially when engaging households with poor literacy in bureaucratic processes. This is particularly relevant for social grants – for instance, the take-up rate for the Child Support Grant is only 60% (Leibbrandt et al., 2010). Overcoming informational problems should be prioritised as they can be resolved relatively cheaply, and because improving the coverage of existing grants should complement other public objectives such as better education and health.

Finally, corruption appears to be an increasingly important barrier to improved public service delivery. South Africa's relative standing on Transparency International's Corruption Perception Index has deteriorated in recent years (Figure 16). Also, voices have

Figure 16. **South Africa's relative position on perceived corruption has worsened**

Percentile rank (higher numbers indicate greater perceived corruption)

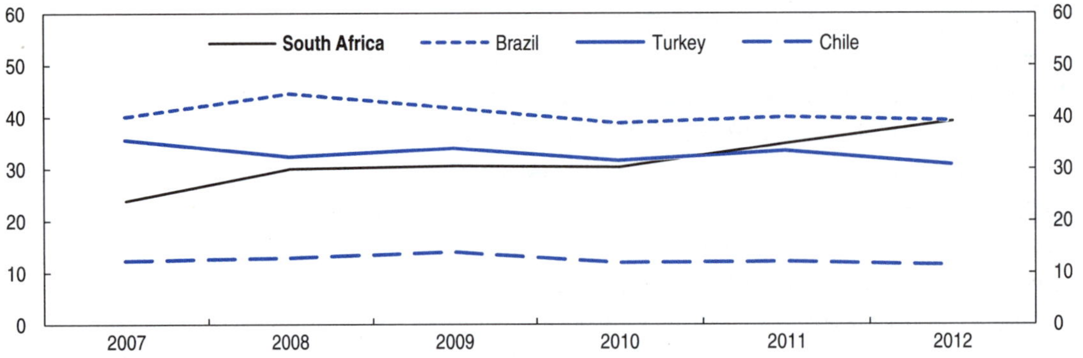

Source: Transparency International, *Corruption Perceptions Indices.*

How to read this figure: The country with the least perceived corruption would be in the first percentile, the country with the most perceived corruption in the 100th percentile.

StatLink ᵃᵍᵖ http://dx.doi.org/10.1787/888932783002

been raised both inside and outside South Africa against the recent law on the protection of state information, which was deemed a setback for press freedom. At the same time, South Africa still ranks well in the areas of budget openness and judicial independence, two public assets that should be safeguarded.

Above all, employment needs to be boosted in both the short and long term

South Africa's employment rate is dismally low. Just over 40% of the working-age population is employed, compared to an OECD average of 65% and similar rates among other middle-income non-OECD economies (Figure 2C). As a consequence, low labour utilisation accounts for about half of the income per capita gap *vis-à-vis* advanced countries. By contrast, in most other middle-income countries virtually all of the gap (and sometimes more than all, where labour utilisation is above OECD levels) is attributable to lower average productivity (Figure 17). South Africa's large labour utilisation gap is largely explained by the low labour force participation rate, which is around 54%, well below the OECD average of 75%. The remainder is accounted for by open unemployment, which was just below 25% in the 4th quarter of 2012 and has been above 20% for 16 years.

There is good evidence that unemployment is overwhelmingly involuntary (Kingdon and Knight, 2001). The share of long-term unemployment (over one year) is disproportionately high (68%), while very few of the unemployed receive unemployment insurance benefits. Indeed, most of the unemployed have never held a job before. In many emerging market economies the informal economy plays an important role in lifting people out of poverty, but in South Africa it represents a relatively small proportion (less than 20%) of total employment.

Unemployment is characterised by two polarising dimensions: age and ethnicity. Unemployment is catastrophically high among youth (51% in the fourth quarter of 2012), compared to 22% for prime-age adults (aged 25-54) and less than 8% for senior workers (55-64). Differences among population groups are also striking, with the unemployment rate at 28½ per cent among Africans compared to 5½ per cent for Whites. This gap can be explained by various factors including differences in educational attainment and education quality, location and household composition, but there is a residual effect which is often interpreted as enduring discrimination on the labour market.

Figure 17. **Much of South Africa's income gap *vis-à-vis* OECD countries is explained by labour utilisation**

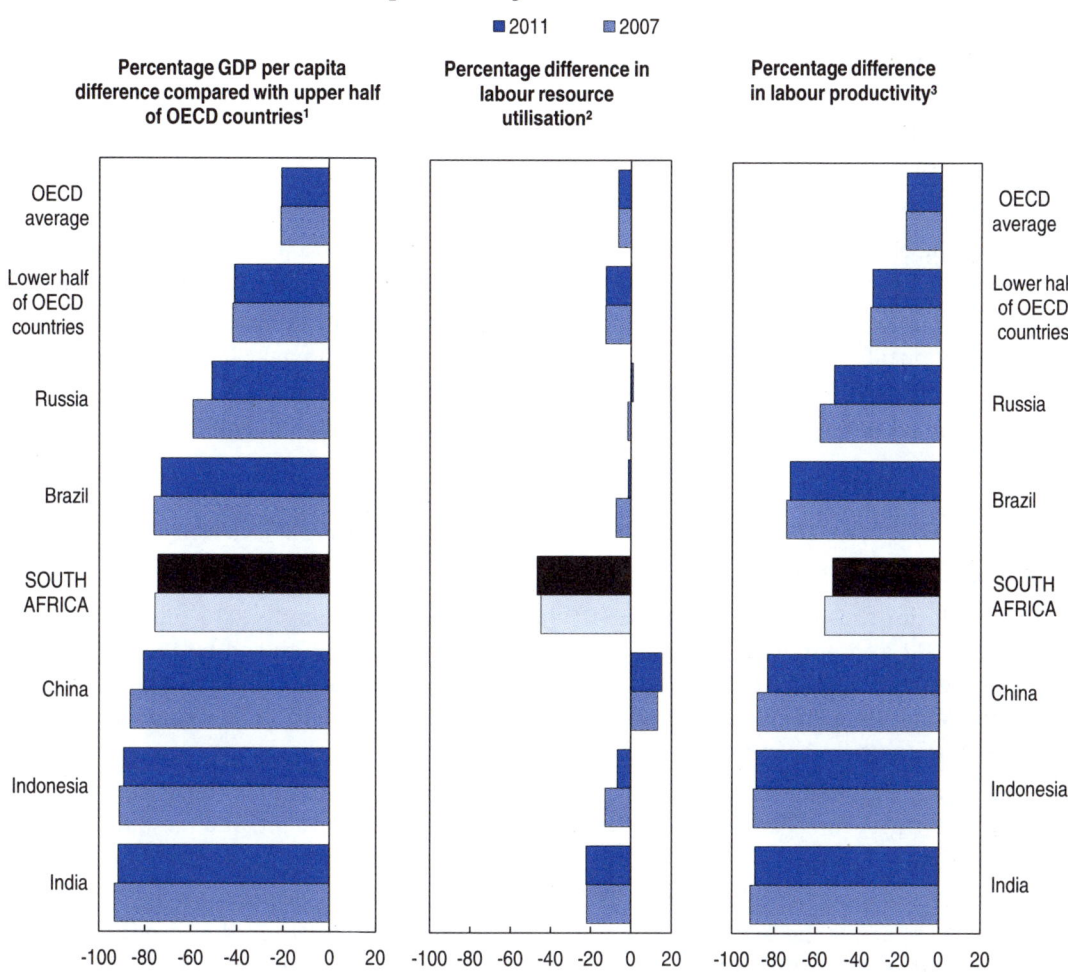

1. Compared to the average of the highest 17 OECD countries in terms of GDP per capita in 2011 and 2007, based on 2011 and 2007 purchasing power parities (PPPs). The OECD average is based on a simple average of the 34 member countries. The sum of the percentage gap in labour resource utilisation and labour productivity does not add up exactly to the GDP per capita gap since the decomposition is multiplicative.
2. Labour resource utilisation is measured as employment as a share of population.
3. Labour productivity is measured as GDP per employee.
Source: OECD (2013), *Going for Growth.*

StatLink 🔗 http://dx.doi.org/10.1787/888932783021

The government's strategic plans are broadly sound, but implementation will be challenging

Recent national strategy documents rightly focus on employment growth

Raising the employment rate is central to both the New Growth Path (NGP), the government's economic strategy through 2020, and the National Development Plan (NDP), a blueprint for overall social development through 2030 (Box 2). The diagnostic report for the NDP sets out 9 primary challenges, but the first of these was simply and rightly that "Too few people work". For its part, the NGP sets a target of creating 5 million jobs by 2020. Given the starting base for total employment of around 13 million, this target is certainly challenging, but, with an implied compound growth rate of just over 3% a year, within the bounds of realism.

The NDP and NGP both acknowledge the large scale of infrastructure needs in South Africa. The NGP sees the potential of 250 000 additional jobs per year through 2015 arising from public investment in infrastructure in energy, transport, water, communications and housing, while the NDP sets a target of 10% of GDP for public infrastructure investment (including state-owned enterprises). In line with these ambitions, the President announced a massive infrastructure programme in his state of the nation speech in February 2012, with projects to be launched across the country. The programme is to be overseen by the Presidential Infrastructure Coordinating Commission that was created in 2011.

Both the NDP and NGP were, characteristically for South Africa, democratic processes, involving considerable consultation, expert advice and transparency. While both hit many of the right notes as regards the main problems and how to address them, each contains some likely pitfalls, and the failure or lack of follow-through on past plans such as AsgiSA and GEAR from 2006 and 1996 respectively, highlight the danger that in practice the positive impact of the NGP and NDP on economic performance will again be limited.

Box 2. **The National Development Plan and the New Growth Path**

The National Development Plan

The National Development Plan (NDP) is a strategy through 2030 published in August 2012 and endorsed by Cabinet a month later. It was produced by the National Planning Commission (NPC), an entity created by the President in 2010 to undertake a critical analysis of the country's performance since the transition to democracy and develop a long-term plan for the country.

The NPC, chaired by the Minister in the Presidency for National Planning, comprises twenty-five part-time experts drawn largely from outside government, and has a full-time secretariat.

The NPC released a "Diagnostics Report" in June 2011 that identified nine primary challenges facing the economy including the quality of health care and education, inadequate and poorly located infrastructure, corruption, low employment, an over-reliance on natural resources, the uneven quality of public service and spatial and social divides. The "Diagnostics Report" formed the basis of a draft plan which was released in November 2011. After consultations with stakeholders, the plan was revised and a final version released in August 2012.

The central objectives of the NDP are to eradicate poverty and sharply reduce inequality by 2030. The NDP specifies a series of targets that need to be met over the next two decades to achieve these objectives, including the creation of 11 million jobs and average annual real GDP growth of 5.7%. The NDP also outlines an action plan to achieve these targets involving a number of institutional and structural reforms.

The New Growth Path

The New Growth Path (NGP) is an economic framework for the period 2010-20. It was developed by the Economic Development Department (EDD). Like the NPC, the EDD was established after the 2009 general elections. Shortly after its creation, the department was tasked with the creation of a new economic plan to replace the Accelerated Shared Growth Initiative for South Africa (AsgiSA), which had been criticised for failing to deliver jobs and reduce inequality.

> ### Box 2. **The National Development Plan and the New Growth Path** (cont.)
>
> A draft framework was presented to Cabinet in November 2009. This was followed by consultations with national economic ministries, provincial development departments, and other stakeholders, with the final NGP Framework document approved and released by the government in November 2010.
>
> The overriding objective of the NGP is employment. The NGP aims to create 5 million jobs by 2020 by identifying sectors that present employment growth opportunities and developing policies to unlock these opportunities. The NGP draws from and builds-on the Industrial Policy Action Plan II developed by the Department of Trade and Industry. In addition, the NGP, like the NDP, identified various structural and social impediments to faster growth and made recommendations on fostering a more growth-friendly macro- and microeconomic environment.
>
> It is not clear whether structures have yet been established to monitor progress made in achieving the various targets set in the NDP and NGP, and the extent to which, if at all, government departments will be held accountable should they fail to make progress in a achieving the targets.
>
> **The relationship between the NDP and the NGP**
>
> Broadly speaking, the NDP should be seen as encompassing the NGP, since the former is longer-term, broader in scope, and was approved later. The NDP notes that *"The [NGP] and this plan are complementary in the effort to lower costs in the economy, especially as high costs contribute towards limiting employment growth and increase hardship for poor households"*. While the objectives and priorities in the NDP and the NGP appear to be broadly consistent, there are some differences in emphasis, with the NGP having a somewhat more interventionist slant, with a greater emphasis on industrial policy. The NDP alludes to this in noting that *"With regard to current government policies and programmes, the New Growth Path is the government's key programme to take the country onto a higher growth trajectory. The New Growth Path is about creating the conditions for faster growth and employment through government investment, microeconomic reforms that lower the costs of business (and for poor households), competitive and equitable wage structures, and the effective unblocking of constraints to investment in specific sectors. The proposals in [the NDP] are largely consistent with these policies. They do, however, cover a longer time frame and the emphasis on catalysts and action steps may differ in some respects."*

The NGP takes a "job engineering" approach taken to charting the targeted employment growth, identifying 10 key sectors and evaluating the scope for job gains in each, which sum up to the targeted 5 million over 10 years. Such an approach might be useful as a communication device, but analytically it would seem preferable to identify market and government failures which may be preventing faster growth and consider how best to overcome them via policy interventions. Plausible market failures could include capital constraints (*e.g.* as regards financing education and training), information imperfections (*e.g.* concerning the returns to boosting energy efficiency), co-ordination problems (*e.g.* in wage-setting), efficiency wage as well as insider-outsider problems (characterising labour markets), and the existence of natural monopolies. As concerns government failures, important issues include barriers to entry in network industries, infrastructure bottlenecks and shortcomings in public service delivery, including corruption.

The NDP is an impressively comprehensive and thoughtful blueprint for a prosperous, safe, democratic South Africa in 2030, with a detailed diagnosis of the many policy challenges. Even though many of the specifics are missing, necessarily so for a long-term strategic document of this sort, the very breadth of the plan risks overtaxing the available implementation capacity. As the NDP itself acknowledges, the administrative capacity of government at all levels is stretched, and this points to the risk of having too diffuse a focus and/or too interventionist an approach. One of the strengths of the now-superseded AsgiSA strategy was that it identified a few bottlenecks to faster development and focussed on easing those constraints via a limited number of policy interventions.

Achieving full employment will be a long and complex task

The low employment rate has many interacting causes, as discussed at greater length in Chapter 3 of the 2010 *Economic Survey of South Africa* (OECD, 2010a). On the labour supply side, deficiencies in education and training, as well as brain drain, have contributed to skill mismatches, a surge of labour force participation among the young and women from the mid-1990s had adverse compositional effects, and the high incidence of HIV/AIDS sapped the capacity of some of the unemployed for active search. There is also a question of whether the expansion of social grants weakened job-search incentives, although the available evidence is mixed and most the expansion came since 2000, by which time the unemployment rate had already risen to the mid-20s.

The greatest problems, however, appear to have been on the demand side of the labour market (Kingdon and Knight, 2007). Above all, economic growth has been insufficiently vigorous to absorb the growing labour supply; when growth rates did pick up, between 2004 and 2008, the unemployment rate declined substantially. Moreover, the elasticity of employment with respect to growth has been low, as labour-intensive mining and manufacturing have shed jobs over a long period. This reflected not only a normal shift towards services but also a secular deterioration in export performance, which in turn was attributable to a combination of currency overvaluation and downward real wage rigidity in the traded goods sector. The informal labour market was prevented from playing a full shock-absorbing role in part by potential barriers to entry or hidden costs in informal employment (Chandra et al., 2002). In particular, land and credit constraints, the suppression of entrepreneurial skills in the African population under apartheid and high crime rates have all conspired against the emergence of a vibrant informal sector and have held back labour demand (Devey et al., 2003).

Unsurprisingly, such a multi-faceted problem will need a multi-pronged strategy, implemented over a long period, to resolve it (OECD, 2010a). As described above, macroeconomic policies should be co-ordinated to eliminate the slack in the economy and avoid prolonged periods of overvaluation of the rand. Improvements in education will be needed to reduce skill mismatches and provide decent jobs for all workers in the longer term. A further expansion of high-density urban housing and public transport networks would help to reduce the spatial misallocation of the population inherited from the apartheid era. Credit constraints for small and medium-sized enterprises should be eased and supporting infrastructure improved, especially in poor areas. Land and water reform must move forward more quickly to give poor rural households access to productive assets. There are also measures to be taken, however, to improve the functioning of labour markets and their interaction with product markets.

Labour markets are sharply dualised, with a relatively small formal private sector in which large unions bargain with large firms, setting high wages that in many cases are extended to other firms in the sector by bargaining councils (Bhorat et al., 2012). This tends to put smaller firms at a disadvantage and deter entry. Exemptions are possible, and the extent to which SMEs are affected has been questioned (Godfrey *et al.*, 2006; World Bank, 2012c), but Magruder (2012) estimates that sectoral bargaining agreements in South Africa decrease employment in affected industries by 8-13%, with losses concentrated among small firms. This is qualitatively consistent with findings on the impact of administrative extension in OECD economies (de Serres and Murtin, 2013). The resultant pattern is that large incumbent firms earn rents which are shared with the labour market insiders fortunate enough to have those jobs. Government is another privileged sector with powerful unions and a less binding budget constraint on the employer. The workers excluded from the primary market to some extent find employment in the less-well-paid secondary market, including the informal sector and subsistence agriculture, although owing to constraints on the development of this secondary market (including limited access to credit and land as well as the prevalence of crime), millions are stuck in unemployment.

A key to improving the functioning of the labour market is to find ways to ensure that collective bargaining reflects the interests of a wider range of workers than at present. One way of doing that would be to reduce the extent to which bargaining is determined at the sectoral level. As argued in the previous *Economic Survey*, a more co-ordinated process, with a role for government to ensure that the interests of the unemployed are also represented, would probably result in better employment outcomes. Evidence from OECD countries (de Serres and Murtin, 2013) suggests that labour market performance tends to be better where the gap between union membership and the number of workers covered by collective bargaining is small. The most obvious way of reducing this gap in South Africa is to narrow the scope for administrative extension of collective bargains in sectors covered by bargaining councils.

The scale of youth inactivity – 31.6% of those aged 15-24 were not in employment, education or training in the 4th quarter of 2012 – and the fact that the negative externalities of long-term unemployment are particularly acute for the young mean that youth-specific measures should be an important part of the strategy to raise employment. As argued in the 2010 *Economic Survey*, a youth wage subsidy, possibly building on the existing learnership programme, should be implemented, together with expanded job search assistance and a differentiation of sectoral minimum wages by age to make it easier for the young to break into the job market. In addition, programmes to develop entrepreneurship among the young in disadvantaged groups should be expanded.

It is also important that policy measures to address problems in the labour market not hamper employment growth. Notably, the use of labour brokers for temporary employment has been associated with violations of labour law, but temporary employment has accounted for a large share of employment growth in recent years, and relatively liberal legislation provisions regarding temporary contracts is one reason why South Africa's Employment Protection Legislation Index is scored as less restrictive than most OECD countries (Figure 18). Depending on the final form of legislation now before parliament and how it is implemented, there is a danger that reforms to temporary employment will reduce flexibility. It would be preferable to focus on curbing abuses of existing laws and avoiding making the regulation of temporary employment more restrictive than necessary to avoid the systematic substitution of regular contracts by non-standard labour contracts.

Since the existence of product market rents appears to be a significant factor behind the persistently poor labour market outcomes, product market reforms also have an important

Figure 18. **Employment protection legislation is relatively liberal**

2008, scale from 0 (least restrictions) to 6 (most restrictions)

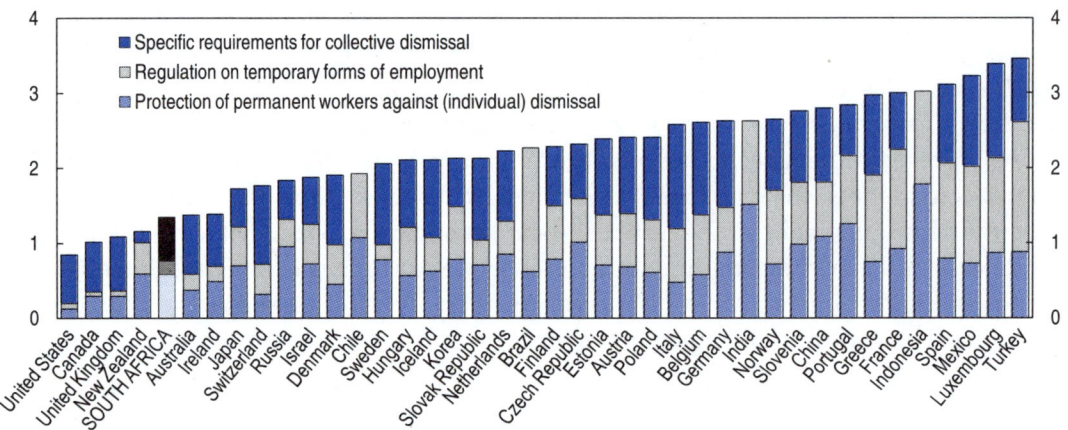

- ■ Specific requirements for collective dismissal
- □ Regulation on temporary forms of employment
- ▨ Protection of permanent workers against (individual) dismissal

Note: Data are for 2009 for France and Portugal.
Source: OECD Indicators on Employment Protection.

StatLink *http://dx.doi.org/10.1787/888932783040*

role to play in boosting employment. As shown in the 2008 *Economic Assessment of South Africa* (OECD, 2008a), product market regulation is relatively restrictive (Figure 19), mainly due to the administrative burden on firms as well as the involvement of the state in business as the owner of network industries. Apart from network industries, the banking industry is another example of high concentration. To some extent this is the flip-side to the admirable stability of the financial system and the narrow base of lending. Weak competitive pressures may allow banks to enjoy comfortable levels of profitability without having to broaden lending to riskier enterprises and individuals. An intensification of competition in banking would probably help to spread financial services more broadly through the economy.

Limited action has been taken to date with respect to past *Survey* recommendations on product market liberalisation (Annex 1). The main thrust of reforms must be to strengthen competition. As argued in previous *Surveys*, possible useful steps to that end would be to expand the powers and resources of the Competition Commission, further liberalise the foreign trade and investment regimes, and avoid a muddling of competition policy with other objectives. In addition, the complexity of regulation should be reduced, such as by increasing the use of one-stop-shops for permits and licenses, and the use of regulatory impact analysis should be expanded to cover all new legislation as well as reviewing existing laws. It will also be important to foster greater competition in network industries via reduced barriers to entry and an unbundling of the functions of the state-owned energy utility Eskom and the transport conglomerate Transnet.

The challenge to push the South African economy onto a more inclusive, labour-intensive and environmentally sustainable growth path along the lines of the strategic government plans becomes easier if economic agents can rely on open markets for new suppliers, functioning infrastructure to facilitate job search and greater freedom for firms and workers to agree on wages. Higher employment will most likely come along with a wider wage distribution, but will also provide better opportunities for learning by doing, further education on the job and participation in innovation activities, all of which will foster career prospects and higher pay. While the current strategy, involving low employment, high wages and high entry barriers, may have been unavoidable in the democratic transition period, an

Figure 19. **Product market regulation is relatively restrictive**

2008, index scale of 0-6 from least to most restrictive

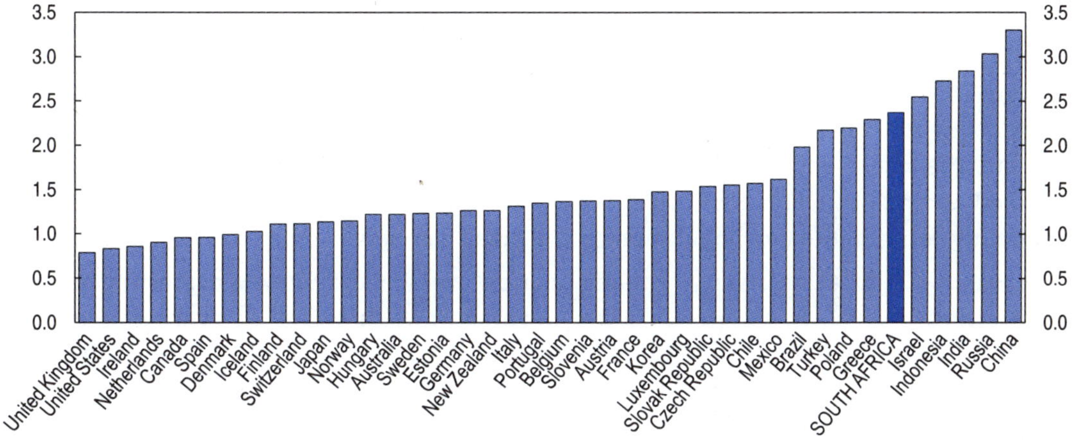

Source: OECD (2011), *Product Market Regulation Database.*

StatLink ⬛ http://dx.doi.org/10.1787/888932783059

approach, which rests on entrepreneurship, job creation and skills formation has a better chance to make economic activity more dynamic and inclusive.

Box 3. Main recommendations for increasing employment

Raising the employment rate and absorbing the excess supply of labour, especially unskilled labour, is a long-term project with coherent action needed on many fronts, with important roles for macroeconomic, education, health, land, water, housing and transport policies. As regards the functioning of the labour market and its interaction with product markets, however, the following steps would be helpful.

Labour market institutions

● Curtail the within-sector legal extension of collective bargaining agreements and increase the level of centralisation and co-ordination in collective bargaining to allow for greater influence of outsiders on wages and conditions.

● Implement a broad package of measures for reducing youth unemployment, including a wage subsidy for hiring young job-seekers, age-differentiated minimum wages and support for training young entrepreneurs.

● Protect the flexibility of temporary employment while addressing abuses of labour law.

Product market regulation

● Make product market regulation less restrictive, particularly as regards barriers to entrepreneurship. Simplify regulations and ease compliance.

● Strengthen competition by expanding the powers and resources of the Competition Commission, further liberalising the foreign trade and investment regimes, and avoiding a muddling of competition policy with other objectives.

● Foster greater competition in network industries via reduced barriers to entry and an unbundling of the functions of Eskom and Transnet.

● Expand the use of regulatory impact analysis to cover all new legislation as well as reviewing existing laws.

Improving basic education is critical for achieving the government's development objectives

South Africa has made sustained educational progress over the past two decades. The South African Schools Act of 1996 made schooling mandatory until age 15 or grade 9, and the goal of full enrolment at primary and lower secondary has been nearly achieved. In 2004 about 89% of the population aged over 15 years and 98% of those aged 15-24 were literate. The formal educational attainment of the African population has been particularly marked and has converged with respect to Whites, as the relative gap in mean years of schooling between the two population groups has been halved since the end of apartheid.

However, education quality remains poor on average and uneven across regions and population groups. South Africa's low performance in terms of average scores in international tests (PIRLS and TIMSS) and regional surveys (SACMEQ) reflects the large fraction of students who do not reach basic qualification standards. The national pass rate in the high-school graduation examination (the "matric"), was 57% among Africans and 99% among Whites in 2009 (Department of Basic Education, 2010). Moreover, the net enrolment rate in primary education has been falling since 1995, pointing to a significant rate of grade repetition and an increasing incidence of out-of-school children of primary school age (World Bank, 2012b). Educational attainment and quality are also unevenly distributed across regions, depending largely on urbanisation rates. While the percentage of children aged 7-15 attending compulsory basic education is broadly the same across regions, gross enrolment rates in secondary vary widely. There are two complementary strategies to overcome the legacy of the past: improving the functionality of the education system mainly through procedural reforms and easing resource constraints in specific areas.

The quality of education can be improved by making better use of available resources

Poor educational outcomes can partly be explained by major dysfunctions largely inherited from the apartheid era. Notable among these is a lack of capacity, in sub-national administrations, schools and teaching. Provincial administrations have on occasion had to be taken under national control. Poor teacher quality has been a particularly serious problem, especially in rural areas, where teachers are frequently absent, and where curriculum coverage is often incomplete. Teachers' own capacities and subject knowledge have been put in doubt by the results of formal tests. In general, the failure on the part of teachers and principals to carry out required tasks has been made possible by a lack of accountability and support.

Ensuring a properly functioning education system with available resources is a priority in the recent "Action Plan to 2014" and many mutually reinforcing measures have been initiated. Overall, South Africa seems to be on track to install a functional school evaluation system. Among OECD countries, successful efficiency-oriented strategies have generally been structured around three self-reinforcing objectives: evaluating the performance of all actors in the education system; improving outcomes by providing constructive feedback and professional development for under-performing teachers and school principals; and adapting the curriculum to provide a better match between educational content and local labour market conditions.

There are various ways of increasing accountability at the administrative and school levels:

● The capacity and regulatory powers of the recently-created federal evaluation unit (NEEDU) could be bolstered to ensure that school, district and provincial authorities are evaluated regularly.

● Failing school principals could be granted training and further surveillance and in the worst cases dismissed.

● Provincial administrations, when proved functional, may be given power to appoint and dismiss school principals, rather than simply block their nomination. The public posting of information on school outcomes at grades 3 and 6 was initiated only recently and in practice there appears often to be a lack of effective pressure from parents on school management. School assessments could be made more publicly widespread, easier to interpret and involve comparisons with other schools provincially and nationally.

The recent implementation of Annual National Assessments, first run in 2008, the provision of "systemic studies" and the requirement for school leaders to provide school development plans all constitute crucial innovations to be maintained and supported by additional capacity-building to analyse these data. At the international level, it would be useful for South Africa to join the OECD's PISA and TALIS surveys to monitor progress and benefit, on an ongoing basis, from the possibility to carry out comparable policy relevant studies in the field of education.

Assessing school principals ultimately serves the purpose of improving school outcomes. As recognised in the Action Plan to 2014, maintaining the right balance between monitoring and support is essential. School principal positions could be made more selective by requiring specific leadership certificates and specific training delivered at the national level. Similarly, the management capacity of incumbent school principals should be upgraded by increasing participation in the university-based Advanced Certificate of Education (ACE) programme. Establishing local networks of school principals and mentoring between well-experienced and new school principals are strongly encouraged (OECD, 2008b), as such practices are deemed to foster the local diffusion of good management practices. In the same vein, twinning schools with different socio-economic context could favour the diffusion of best pedagogical practices from well-performing to low-performing schools. Finally, providing more support staff to schools would allow teachers to spend more time on teaching. At least some support staff could be hired by the Community Work Programme, which is already budgeted.

Teacher-related reforms should aim at suppressing teacher absenteeism, simplifying teacher evaluation and improving teaching quality. Addressing teacher absenteeism by enforcing daily monitoring in less functional schools is a first important requirement that would again be facilitated by the provision of additional administrative and support staff. Recent evidence shows that only 17% of schools maintain up-to-date daily educator attendance registers (Action Plan to 2014, p. 137, Department of Basic Education, 2011).

As with school principals, teacher assessment should ultimately seek to improve teaching quality. All teachers could be evaluated mainly through annual assessments by their principals, who would themselves become accountable for these assessments via government audits. Teacher peer reviews may also be encouraged, but it would seem premature to use students' performance in national and standardised tests as an important criterion for teacher evaluation. In addition, the frequency, content and place of instruction of teacher training could be jointly reviewed by evaluation authorities and unions with the aim of emphasising training quality over quantity. Professional development could be based on needs identified through teacher evaluations rather than taking place, as now, in an automatic (and frequent) way. This would free up resources to improve subject knowledge of teachers with an incomplete curriculum.

Regarding wage incentives, teachers with low pay appear to be much better off than low-paid South-Africans, but teachers with high wages are worse off than South African high-wage earners (van der Berg and Burger, 2010). Consequently, the government is rightly considering hiring primary teachers without university qualification, who should nevertheless be qualified enough to teach in Foundation Phase. Secondly, wage increases for the best teachers who pass formal examinations of subject knowledge are being examined (Department of Basic Education, 2011). Such increases should be applied in a very selective way to ensure containment of the teacher wage bill, and should target the best teachers working in disadvantaged and remote areas, which are the most affected by teacher shortages.

Adapting the curriculum to local needs is another area where efficiency gains could be realised. Large disparities in administrative capacity suggest that it would not be a good idea to generalise curriculum autonomy and decentralisation in an unconditional manner, as international evidence suggests that such decentralisation is only effective in mature education systems, and can lead to poor outcomes when local institutions lack capacity or when an operative accountability system is not in place. However, tailoring the curriculum to local conditions and/or by school quintiles would help to improve the match between educational content and local needs. For instance, greater emphasis on basic skills such as reading, writing and arithmetic is recommended in low-performing schools in Finland, one of the best performers in PISA tests.

In addition, there is widespread evidence that pupils with an African mother tongue perform significantly worse in English than first-language Afrikaans or English speakers. It would therefore seem desirable to strengthen the teaching of English as a second language in African-language schools, in part by introducing it earlier, at primary and pre-primary school level. At the same time, the switch in the main language of instruction from mother tongue to English, which theoretically happens currently at grade 4, appears to be abrupt and confusing for African students. International evidence (OECD, 2012b) suggests that it could be useful to make the switch to English as the language of instruction more gradually. Finally, making it easier for English teachers from other (English-speaking) countries to immigrate, or allowing Zimbabwean teachers already living in South Africa to teach, would help to address pressing and immediate teacher shortages.

Expenditure should be distributed in a more equitable way and increased in specific areas

Although total educational resources as a share of GDP are in line with OECD standards, they do not fully match the needs of South Africa's large school-age population, especially in poor and rural areas. In 2010, total public expenditures on educational institutions and administration amounted to 5.9% of GDP, above the OECD average of 5.4% (World Bank, 2012b and OECD, 2012c). However, when calculated per pupil and normalised by a proxy for income (GDP per capita), resources spent on pupils at primary and secondary levels are about 30% lower than the OECD average (Figure 20A and B). The share of public expenditure on capital has been very low (Figure 20C and D), in contrast to expenditures on

Figure 20. **The education system needs more teachers and more capital**
2009 data

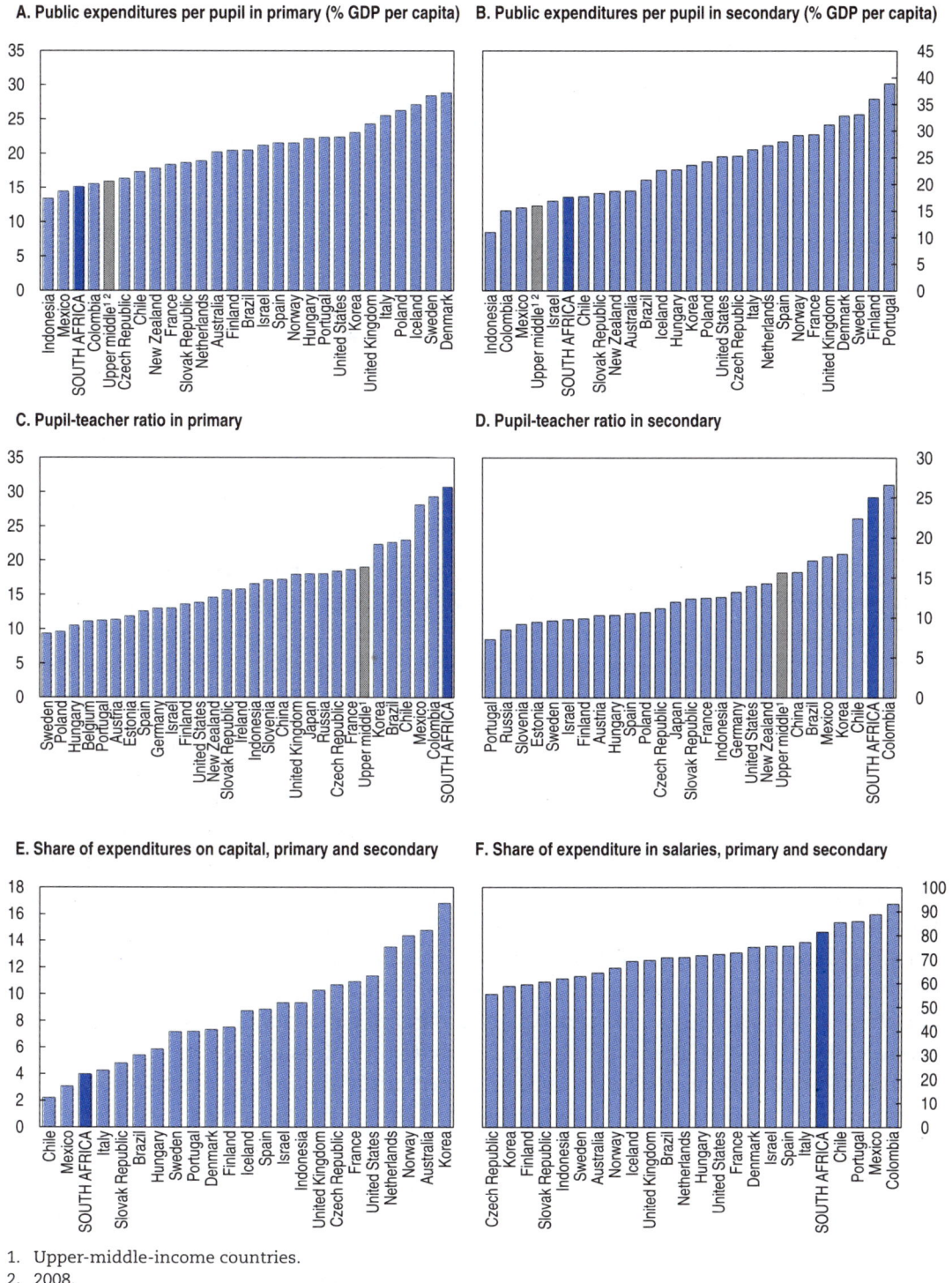

1. Upper-middle-income countries.
2. 2008.
Source: World Bank (2012), *Online Education Statistics.*

StatLink ᴬᴵˢᴸ http://dx.doi.org/10.1787/888932783078

personnel. A rebalancing of the budget towards basic facilities (textbooks, school infrastructure through the 'ASIDI' programme) and ICT availability, which would offer access to information and communication infrastructure to children from poor households, is a declared and welcome objective of the Action Plan to 2014 (Department of Basic Education, 2011). Empirical analysis using a large sample of South African pupils at grade 9 (see Chapter 1) shows that the impact of school equipment (libraries and ICT in particular) on pupils' test scores is as large as the influence of parental socio-economic background.

Beyond school infrastructure, there is a clear shortage of teachers in primary and secondary schools, as reflected by very high pupil-teacher ratios (Figure 20E and F). Moreover, teacher shortages are similarly observed at the secondary level. The provision of additional teachers is a difficult challenge, which can be overcome only over the medium term through a dramatic expansion of the pool of new teachers and the containment of teacher salaries, although the prospective reduction in the number of students due to demographic shifts will help reduce class size conditionally on maintaining a constant number of teachers. As there is evidence of important credit constraints for undertaking upper secondary and university studies, fostering the expansion of conditional bursary schemes to become a teacher (through "*Funza Lushaka*" schemes) would be a promising way to raise both the quantity and the quality of young teachers over the next decade.

Public expenditure on education is still distributed inequitably despite bold action to mitigate the consequences of the past. Before 1994, funding was skewed towards the former White schools by a factor of 5 to 1. The introduction of a rule to calculate an "equitable" budget allocation per pupil ("Equitable Share Formula") and the more recent use of national quintiles to fund schools in a progressive way ("National Norms and Standards for School Funding") sought to address the stark socio-economic inequality perpetuated at school.

Yet the education system remains dualistic, with on the one hand a small number of former White schools that can collect tuition fees to supplement teaching and other resources, and on the other hand "no-fee" schools that rely entirely on government funds, do not have enough teachers and generally perform poorly. Whereas school fees are only 7% of all school resourcing, they constitute a much larger share of financing of good schools. Moreover, fee-charging schools are subsidised by the government for each disadvantaged child exempted from paying fees, which on the one hand means that already relatively well-resourced schools get an additional advantage. At the same time, however, since the subsidy is typically much less than the fees charged to other students, additional pitfalls arise, such as a lack of information about their rights among poor parents or non-compliance of school management with their obligation to accept non-fee-paying students.

There are two ways to reduce the duality of the basic education system. One is to phase out school fees gradually so as to avoid a collapse of the best-performing schools and a massive flight to private schools. Another is to increase the redistribution of school funding providing that schools are classified adequately by child socio-economic status rather than school geographical location as it is currently the case.

Making educational investments pay

Empirical analysis presented in Chapter 1 points to large employability premiums and high private returns to tertiary education and to high school graduation (passing the matric). While returns are lower for the African population relative to Whites, part of the latter gap reflects differences in school quality as measured by pupil-teacher ratios. Raising and levelling out education quality standards would therefore contribute to lower income inequality and raise both private and social returns to education.

The high youth unemployment rate highlights the issue of skills deficiencies among those who fail to pass the matric exam. From that perspective, the vocational education and training system appears to be underdeveloped and not functioning as an alternative for high-school drop-outs. Further Education and Training (FET) colleges represent less than 10% of pupils enrolled at secondary schools, and display by far the highest pupil-teacher ratios in the education system. In practice, technical colleges are characterised by high churn rates as students often drop out and return. Moreover, the pool of students in vocational education is often considered to be of lower quality. Successful vocational education and training (VET) systems in OECD countries often both provide a path to higher education, which raises the quality of new entrants, and offer a strong connection to the labour market thanks to up-to-date curricula in tune with labour market needs.

It is necessary to raise both the demand for and the supply of skilled students with a vocational degree. On the demand side, there is still too little on-the-job training for VET students in spite of recent action taken in this area, as firms may be reluctant to engage in burdensome administrative procedures. The VET system would benefit from simplified administrative procedures to hire trainees and from tax credits for firms that provide training. On the supply side, the VET system barely delivers the skills needed as its curriculum is deemed to be outdated, with shortcomings in the quality of both lecturers and infrastructure. Recent initiatives involving better participation of firms in the definition of the curriculum are especially welcome. Moreover, developing partnerships between large companies and public or private FET colleges is a powerful way of raising the quality of the system. Several foreign companies have been involved in this kind of arrangement, unlike large domestic firms. To complement this, expanding the bursary system in well-identified segments of the VET system, such as those linked to booming economic sectors, would simultaneously help raise the quality of applicants while fulfilling strategic skill development needs of the country.

Focusing on a specific part of the vocational system, the expansion of the apprenticeship system, may be a useful tool to reduce youth unemployment. Restoring an effective apprenticeship system is an explicit goal of the New Growth Path, which plans for the training of 50 000 additional artisans by 2014-15. Among OECD countries, well-functioning apprenticeship systems often have the following characteristics: students' pay is usually a fraction of the minimum wage, but in exchange they receive recognised skills from experienced supervisors and part-time schooling of usually not more than 2 days per week. The curriculum is established with the active participation of social partners, and Economics Departments/Ministries are usually co-responsible for such programmes. The attraction for the employer is not only the availability of cheap labour during the time of the programme (usually 3-4 years), but also the prospect of having privileged access to tailor-skilled graduates. Except for the schooling part of the programme, public funds are usually provided only if companies agree to train more apprentices than they would want to keep at the end or when companies provide a training infrastructure for students who are not in employment, education or training (OECD, 2012d; Box 2.3).

Box 4. **Main recommendations on education**

● Expand the Accelerated Schools Infrastructure Development Initiative programme to address infrastructure backlogs and improve the delivery of learning materials (textbooks, desks, libraries and computers) with priority to the most deprived schools.

● Expand the *Funza Lushaka* bursary programme for teaching studies and allow more immigration of English teachers.

● Provide more school leadership training and support staff in exchange for stricter accountability. Allow the education authorities to appoint and dismiss school principals in a more flexible way (depending on progress on school performance in Annual National Assessments and on external reviews), while making school principals responsible for yearly teacher evaluations and monitoring teachers' daily attendance.

● Empower the independent federal evaluation unit NEEDU, join the Programme for International Student Assessment (PISA) and the Teaching and Learning International Survey (TALIS) and undertake an OECD *Review of Evaluation and Assessment Frameworks for Improving School Outcomes*.

● Focus on teacher training on low-performers and subject knowledge.

● Expand the "no fee school policy" and reclassify schools according to median learners' socio-economic background rather than school location to improve the effectiveness of redistribution.

● Foster on-the-job training with tax credits and simplify administrative procedures for hiring trainees from FET colleges. Widen the scope for apprenticeship programmes organised by public-private partnerships.

Greener growth is needed for sustainability

The aim of faster growth should be met within a strategy for environmental sustainability

As noted in the NDP, for more than a century South Africa exploited its natural resources including water with little regard for the environmental consequences. It has increasingly been realised that this approach must change and that it will only be possible to get sustained rapid inclusive growth if policies are also geared to limiting environmental harm in an efficient way.

The authorities are aware of the need to tackle key environmental challenges and have increasingly embraced green growth policies. In the South African context, where employment creation is a critical priority, there is an understandable emphasis on the scope for job creation in the "green economy". The NGP, for example, provides measures for the creation of 300 000 green jobs by 2020.

While focussing on the "green economy" and "green jobs" may be useful to garner support for green policies, the main rationale for using policy interventions to promote greener growth is that since various environmental harms (such as carbon emissions) are not reflected in market prices, in the absence of policy interventions such harms will be oversupplied and the well-being of the population will be lower. While it is realistic to hope that, given substantial idle resources, achieving greener growth can also contribute to raising employment, one risk of playing up the jobs-boosting potential of green activities is that it may lead to a muddling of objectives, with green growth initiatives being judged mainly on their perceived employment potential rather than their contribution (and the cost effectiveness of that contribution) to sustained growth in well-being. It may also detract attention from the many other policy measures needed to deliver satisfactory growth rates: notably, promoting competition, improving the functioning of the labour market, maintaining the right macroeconomic policy mix and creating favourable framework conditions for investment and innovation.

An important aspect of assessing costs and benefits of green growth policies and evaluating their results is having sufficient data on different aspects of the problem. As called for in the NDP, it will be important for South Africa to expand its efforts to monitor a range of environmental outcomes. One useful direction would be for Statistics South Africa to work towards the development of national accounts measures that factor in natural resource depletion and the costs of environmental degradation, although such efforts are in their infancy even in more developed countries. More immediately, South Africa could look to monitor a limited set of Headline Indicators along with a broader range of measures, as proposed in the OECD's Green Growth Indicators (OECD, 2011a, 2012e). There is also a need for more accurate and detailed monitoring of water use and greenhouse gas emissions to establish baselines and inform policy.

South Africa faces environmental policy challenges in a range of areas, including waste management, local air and water pollution, pressures on biodiversity and marine resource management. The forthcoming OECD Environmental Performance Review will address the full panoply of environmental issues. Among the most pressing policy questions, however, are those relating to climate change mitigation and water use management, and the focus of this Survey (Chapter 2) is on these areas. In both cases, the authorities are working towards the expanded use of pricing of externalities to encourage a more economically efficient use of resources, but face important challenges of implementation in the context of a pressing need for action.

Greater efforts will be needed to meet the government's climate change mitigation commitments

South Africa's economy is energy-intensive and overly reliant on coal for electricity generation. This in part reflects natural endowments, both as regards coal but also the abundance of other minerals, with the mining value-chain being energy intensive. But that factor has been reinforced by a long period of underpricing of both electricity and coal. Electricity is much less underpriced than it was, after a series of sharp rises since 2008, but South Africa still has among the lowest prices internationally (Figure 21) and the current price remains well below the full marginal costs of Eskom, to say nothing of higher-cost renewables.

Coal for electricity generation has also long been priced well below international levels, which has helped to keep electricity prices down and explains the very high share of coal-fired plants in total electricity production (above 90%). Most of the coal produced is sold to power plants in coal-mining areas, while transport bottlenecks have prevented exports from providing strong competitive pressure. The rise in international coal prices in recent years and growing demand from India for South African coal have strengthened the incentive to export, leading to calls from both outside and within government to limit coal

Figure 21. **Electricity prices are still very low by international standards**
2011 or latest year available, USD per MWh

A. Electricity for industry

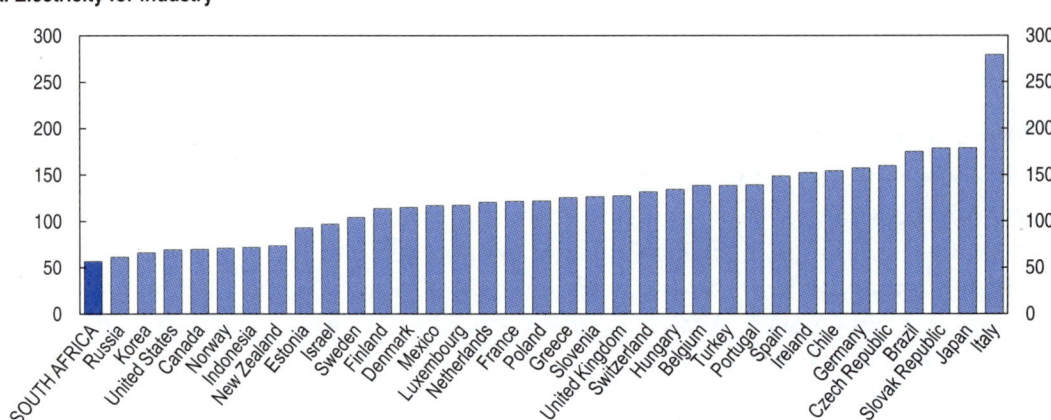

B. Electricity for households

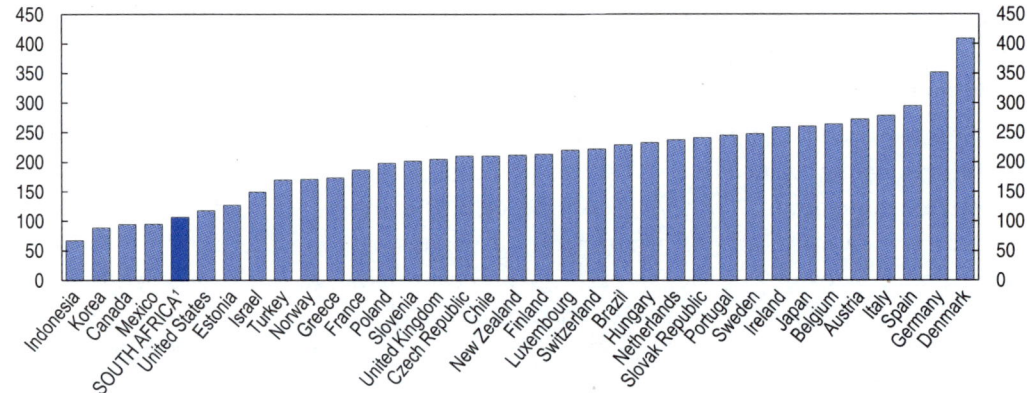

1. Eskom prices for households. Prices set by municipalities are generally higher.
Note: Fiscal year (April 2011-March 2012) for South Africa, 2010 for Korea (industry only), Indonesia, Canada, Estonia and Brazil.
Source: IEA (2012), Energy Prices and Taxes; OECD estimates and Eskom.

StatLink ⋙ http://dx.doi.org/10.1787/888932783097

exports and ensure preferential access for Eskom, which would prolong the subsidisation of domestic coal consumption.

In part as a result of the underpricing of electricity and coal over the last two decades, South Africa has among the highest greenhouse gas emissions per unit of GDP in the world and has seen less decoupling of real GDP and CO_2 emissions in recent years than most other countries (Figure 22). About half of OECD countries achieved positive output growth in the 2000s with an absolute reduction in CO_2 emissions from fuel combustion, whereas in South Africa the percentage increase in emissions was about two thirds of that for real GDP during the same period. This was also higher than for most middle-income non-OECD economies.

The government has been intensifying its efforts to confront the challenge of climate change mitigation. This concern is a major element in the NDP and the NGP, and there have numerous other plans and initiatives, including a National Climate Change Response Policy and a proposal for the introduction of a carbon tax. At the international level, South Africa has articulated a commitment, conditional on the provision of external financing, to

Figure 22. **South Africa has achieved relatively little decoupling of real GDP and CO$_2$ emissions**

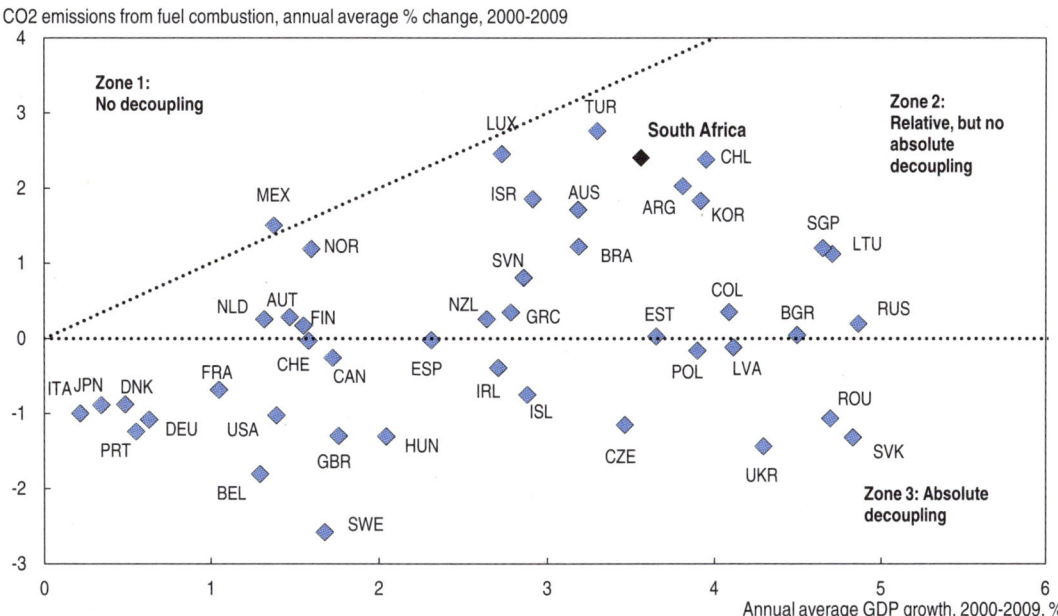

Source: OECD, *National Accounts Database;* World Bank, *WDI online Database;* and IEA (2011), *CO$_2$ emissions from fuel combustion.*

StatLink ᵃᵃˢᵖ *http://dx.doi.org/10.1787/888932783116*

reduce emissions relative to a Business as Usual scenario by 34% by 2020 and 42% by 2025, as its contribution to an international effort to limit warming relative to pre-industrial times to less than 2 degrees Celsius.

It is not clear, however, that the instruments and policies identified to date will deliver an emissions path consistent with that commitment even if fully and promptly implemented. One of the main planks of the approach is the Integrated Resource Plan (IRP), which establishes a development path for electricity production by different sources (coal, gas, nuclear and renewables). But the reduction in power-sector carbon dioxide emissions relative to business as usual implied by the IRP, though substantial (19% by 2025), would leave other sectors having to achieve much deeper emissions cuts. This does not appear plausible under currently identified policies, suggesting that either the IRP will have to be revisited to achieve lower emissions or that additional measures will be needed to get larger emissions reductions elsewhere.

Furthermore, progress towards implementing those policies and instruments has been slow. There is so far no explicit economy-wide carbon price, and putting in place a carbon tax is taking longer than expected. Also, when the carbon tax is put in place, it is expected that the initial rate will be set at a very low level, so that it is likely to be several years before the effect on behaviour is significant. Moreover, progress to date under the IRP is partial: auctioning of renewables capacity has been delayed and plans to install new nuclear capacity by 2023 are beginning to look unrealistic and/or excessively costly.

Thus, with incomplete specification of the instruments that would deliver the targeted emissions profile and uncertain progress to date with the instruments that have been identified, it is all the more essential that policies be implemented effectively and at least cost. For South Africa it appears particularly important, in designing climate change mitigation policies, to bear in mind administrative capacity constraints. This consideration favours instruments such as a simple carbon tax, which is effective but relatively easy to administer, rather than, for example, extensive sectoral carbon budgeting with cap-and-trade or industrial policies driven by subsidies and tax breaks. A suitably simple carbon tax would be uniform, based on the carbon content of fuels, apply to all sectors, eschew border tax adjustments, and avoid earmarking of "recycled" revenues.

Even before ensuring that negative externalities are reflected in prices, however, the most obvious and economically efficient first step towards reducing carbon emissions is to unwind existing incentives to over-consume energy and especially to over-use coal. The most important aspect of this is to ensure that electricity prices fully cover costs, including capital costs, with coal inputs valued at export-parity prices, net of transport costs. This would require further large increases in electricity prices in coming years. A renegotiation of below-cost long-term contracts with industrial users would also enhance efficiency. Another aspect of subsidised pricing is the free provision of electricity to poor districts. Although this relates to a small proportion of total consumption and has clear social benefits (including the reduced use of fuel indoors for heat and light), it may contribute to the problematic culture of non-payment and is poorly targeted - notably, the many households with no connection do not benefit. It could therefore be worthwhile seeking more economically efficient means, such as cash transfers or vouchers, to support poor families. In any case, it will be important to minimise the additional burden on the poorest from the necessary further increase in electricity prices.

Also, the carbon tax should be applied as broadly as possible, including the electricity industry. One argument for exempting electricity production is that the Integrated Resource Plan already imposes an implicit carbon price by requiring higher-cost low-carbon energy sources to be included in the electricity generation mix. Processes and technologies can vary even for given fuel types, however, and applying the carbon tax to electricity generators provides the incentive needed to find less emissions-intensive methods of generation. It could be that including electricity producers in the tax would over time lead to an even lower-carbon mix than provided for in the IRP – for example, it may become more economic to commission gas-fired plants and decommission coal-fired ones. Also, the relative price of electricity would be pushed somewhat higher than otherwise, increasing the incentive for energy-saving by consumers. In any case, given that electricity production accounts for the lion's share of carbon emissions, it will be important to regularly revisit and revise the IRP to take account of new information about technologies, costs and demand.

Apart from broad coverage, it would also be useful for the government to minimise uncertainty about the future path of carbon prices by committing in advance to a given time profile for the carbon tax, in order to facilitate long-term investment decisions and encourage eco-innovation.

South Africa's approach to containing the growth of emissions has so far given too little emphasis to increasing energy efficiency, which at the margin is less costly per unit of emissions reduction than expansion of low-carbon energy supply or de-carbonising fossil fuel combustion (and may also be cheaper even than building new fossil-fuel-based electricity generation). Much of the residential housing stock, particularly public housing, is of poor quality and highly inefficient, while the industrial structure has been skewed towards energy-intensive activities in part by a long history of excessively low electricity prices.

Both these problems can be addressed in part via higher electricity prices, but there is probably also a case for intensifying other policy efforts to raise energy efficiency. Building more energy-efficient social housing and renovation of buildings to increase energy efficiency retrofits can be cost-effective while also generating significant construction employment (OECD 2010b). Construction tends to use low-skilled labour, which is in massive over-supply in South Africa, intensively. Another way in which energy efficiency can be enhanced is through spatial planning, especially in cities. Making urban areas safer and denser, with improved public transport and facilitation of walking and cycling, would help to reduce energy use per unit of GDP and reduce greenhouse gas emissions (OECD, 2010b, 2011b).

Implementation of water management policies is lagging

As a result of its semi-arid climate, South Africa has lower water resources per capita than any OECD country except Israel (Figure 23 – the inner panel magnifies the left-hand part of the outer one). More than 30% of renewable water resources are used, with much higher rates in some catchment areas, and the abstraction rate is projected to rise as a result of increases in population and economic activity as well as the effects of climate change. The increased frequency of extreme weather events, including droughts, will tend to aggravate water stress. Also, coal-fired power plants, on which South Africa relies almost exclusively, are very water-intensive. A successful climate change mitigation policy will therefore contribute to managing the challenge of water stress in the long term.

Figure 23. **Water resources are scarce**

Total renewable water resources per capita (m³/inhab/yr), 2010

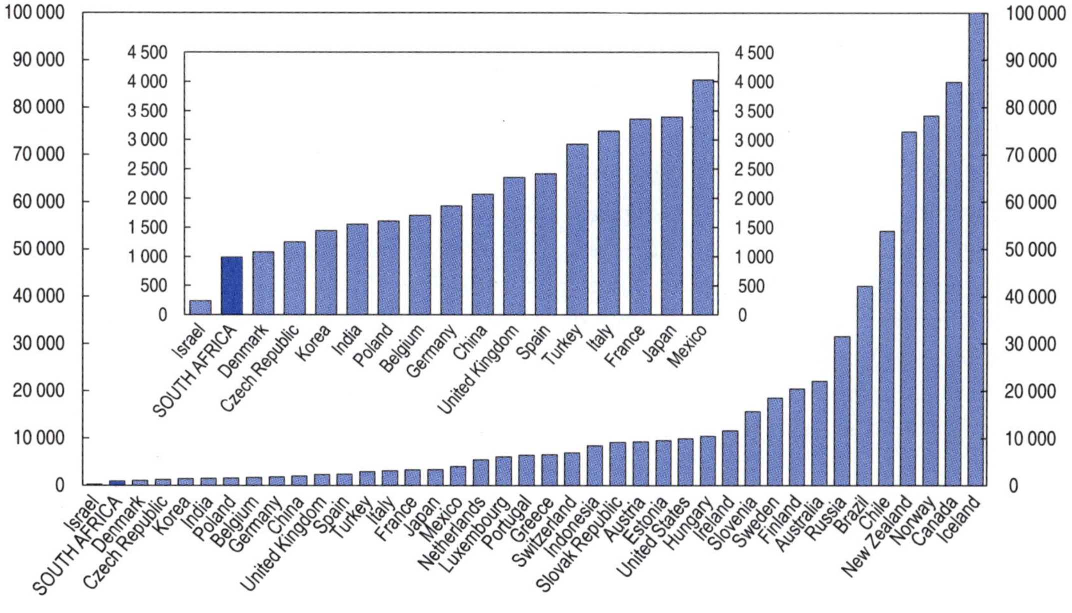

Source: FAO, AQUASTAT Database on line.

StatLink http://dx.doi.org/10.1787/888932783135

Water management policies have been in line with best international practice in design, but dogged by slow and imperfect implementation. A series of laws and strategies in the late 1990s set out the basic approach, which enshrines the user pays and polluter pays principles and adopts the concept of Integrated Water Resources Management in order to reconcile equity, efficiency and sustainability considerations. A part of water resources is designated as the Reserve, which has two components, ecological and social. The ecological component is the amount of unused water necessary to ensure that water use is sustainable, while the social component is to meet the basic needs of the population. In principle, only when the Reserve is met can other water use be authorised, largely under licenses. It was hoped that the trading of allocations under the licenses would put a price on the marginal use of water and help to ensure an efficient use of this limited resource. Increasing block tariffs are used for pricing water supply to households so as to deliver free basic water while providing incentives to limit demand.

In practice, the system has suffered from problems of both efficiency and equity, and in some catchment areas the Reserve is compromised by excessive water use, notwithstanding the theoretical imperative that it be protected. National laws and water strategies have not been applied consistently, and in general water charges have been insufficient to cover maintenance and investment needs, let alone price environmental externalities. This is especially true in agriculture, which, as in many countries, is the main water user. A great deal of agricultural water use goes unmeasured and uncharged, and water charges for agricultural users do not yet reflect full supply costs, which should be rectified. As to retail tariffs, in general tariff-setting entities are self-regulating and there has been little guidance on how to apply the principles governing tariff policy. There may therefore be a case for creating an independent regulator to ensure better and more consistent regulation of retail water tariffs across the country. An important step towards effective regulation would be to require municipalities to separate the accounting of costs and revenues for water and sanitation to improve reporting.

Also, in some cases water allocation bears the inequitable imprint of the apartheid era. For example, while large-scale farmers were often able, because of slow licensing, to continue using water freely, companies that run stand-pipes for poor households that don't have their own water connections have sometimes had to acquire licenses, raising the price paid for basic needs by unconnected households.

Another important challenge is water pollution. While a system for charging for waste discharge was developed nearly a decade ago as an instrument to limit pollution, it has yet to be implemented, and this is an urgent priority. There may also be a case for taxing fertiliser in order to limit diffuse water pollution, which is hard to measure and charge directly. An additional problem is acid mine drainage from old disused mines, which has been revealed to be a significant threat to water quality in major population centres. This has highlighted the need for provisions for mine closure and rehabilitation to be improved.

Box 5. **Main recommendations on achieving greener growth**

Climate change mitigation

- Reduce implicit and explicit subsidies for energy and coal consumption, and use other instruments, such as cash transfers or supply vouchers, for protecting the poor.

- In designing climate change mitigation policies, favour broad and easy-to-implement instruments with limited demands on administrative capacity, such as a simple carbon tax.

> ## Box 5. **Main recommendations on achieving greener growth** (*cont.*)
>
> - Apply the carbon tax as broadly as possible, including the electricity sector.
> - Regularly revisit and revise the Integrated Resource Plan to take account of new information about technologies, costs and demand.
> - Within the approach to emissions mitigation, increase the emphasis on energy efficiency.
> - Give responsibility for monitoring progress on the various objectives relating to climate change to a single institution, and make that institution accountable to parliament via a regular reporting process.
>
> **Water**
>
> - Accelerate the allocation of water-use licenses and ensure that charges for water reflect supply costs and scarcity.
> - Give responsibility for ensuring that water pricing is consistent with national laws and policies to an independent regulator.

Bibliography

van der Berg, S. and R. Burger (2010), "Teacher pay in South Africa", *Stellenbosch University Working Papers*, No. 26/2010.

Bhorat, H., C. van der Westhuizen and S. Goga (2012), "Institutional Wage Effects: Revisiting Union and Bargaining Council Wage Premia in South Africa", *Development Policy Research Unit Working Papers*, No. 12/151, Cape Town.

Chandra, V., Moorty, L., Rajaratnam, B. and K. Schaefer (2002), *"Constraints to Growth and Employment in South Africa. Report 1: Statistics from the Large Manufacturing Survey"*, *World Bank Discussion Papers*, No. 14, World Bank, Washington, DC.

Devey, R., C. Skinner and I. Valodia (2003), "The Informal Economy", Human Resources Development Council, Johannesburg.

Demombynes, G. and B. Özler (2005), "Crime and local inequality in South Africa", *Journal of Development Economics*, Vol. 76(2), pp. 265-292.

Department of Basic Education of South Africa (2010), *Education for All*, Pretoria.

Department of Basic Education of South Africa (2011), *Action Plan to 2014*, Pretoria.

Godfrey, S., J. Maree and J. Theron (2006). "Conditions of Employment and Small Business: Coverage, Compliance and Exemptions", *Development Policy Research Unit Working Papers*, No. 06/106, Cape Town.

IMF (2012), *The Liberalization and Management of Capital Flows: An Institutional View*, IMF, Washington, DC.

Kingdon, G. and J. Knight (2001), "Unemployment in South Africa: the Nature of the Beast", *The Centre for the Study of African Economies Working Paper Series*, No. 153, Centre for the Study of African Economies, *www.bepress.com/csae/paper153*.

Kingdon, G. and J. Knight (2007), "Unemployment in South Africa, 1995–2003: Causes, Problems and Policies", *Journal of African Economies*, Vol. 16(5), pp. 813-848.

Leibbrandt, M., Woolard, I., Finn, A. and J. Argent (2010), "Trends in South African Income Distribution and Poverty since the Fall of Apartheid", OECD Publishing.

Magruder, J. (2012), "High Unemployment Yet Few Small Firms: The Role of Centralised Bargaining in South Africa", *American Economic Journal: Applied Economics*, 2012 Vol. 4(3), pp. 138-166.

Morrisson, C. and F. Murtin (2012), "Vers un Monde Plus Égal?", *Revue d'économie du développement*, Vol. 26(2), pp. 5-30.

OECD (2008a), *Economic Assessment of South Africa*, OECD Publishing.

OECD (2008b), *Reviews of National Policies for Education: South Africa*, OECD Publishing.

OECD (2010a), *OECD Economic Surveys: South Africa 2010*, OECD Publishing.

OECD (2010b), *Cities and Green Growth Conceptual Framework*, OECD Publishing.

OECD (2011a), *Towards Green Growth: Monitoring Progress - OECD Indicators*, OECD Publishing.

OECD (2011b), *Regional Outlook*, OECD Publishing.

OECD (2012a), *Income Distribution and Poverty Income Statistics*, *http://dotstat.oecd.org/Index.aspx*.

OECD (2012b), *Languages in a Global World: Learning for Better Cultural Understanding*, OECD Publishing.

OECD (2012c), *Education at a Glance*, OECD Publishing.

OECD (2012d), *OECD Economic Surveys: Slovak Republic 2012*, OECD Publishing.

OECD (2012e), "Monitoring Progress Towards Green Growth: OECD Headline Indicators", unpublished internal OECD document.

Prasad, E., R. Rajan and A. Subramanian (2007), "Foreign Capital and Economic Growth", *Brookings Papers on Economic Activity*, 2007:1, pp. 153-209.

de Serres, A. and F. Murtin (2013), "Unemployment and the Automatic Extension of Collective Wage Agreements", *Working Papers*, OECD Publishing, forthcoming.

World Bank (2012a). "South Africa Economic Update: Focus on Inequality of Opportunity", *World Bank Working Papers*, No. 71553, World Bank, Washington, DC.

World Bank (2012b). Online Education Statistics. Data available at the following link: *http://databank.worldbank.org/Data/Views/VariableSelection/SelectVariables.aspx?source=Education%20Statistics*.

World Bank (2012c). *World Development Report 2013: Jobs*, World Bank, Washington, DC, DOI:10.1596/978-0-8213-9575-2, License: Creative Commons Attribution CC BY 3.0.

ANNEX 1

Progress on structural reform

This Annex reviews action taken on recommendations from the 2010 *Economic Survey of South Africa*.

Recommendations	Actions taken since the previous *Survey* (July 2010)
Emerging from the crisis	
Further industrial and trade policy interventions based on the effects of the crisis on particular industries should be resisted, and the measures already taken unwound as quickly as possible.	The government has continued to pursue industrial policy interventions aimed at alleviating the impact of weak external demand on particular industries. These include: • The Manufacturing Competitiveness Enhancement Programme, announced early in 2012, provides funding to labour-intensive manufacturing industries, including distressed manufacturers. Treasury has allocated ZAR 5.75 billion over the period 2012/13 and 2015/16 to fund the programme. The programme consists of an investment matching grant component and a working capital funding component which offers loans at preferential rates as well as grant finance. ZAR 2.3 billion has been allocated to the development of Special Economic Zones. The funds will be used largely for infrastructure development, but also to fund incentives to attract private investment into the Zones (although the exact from of investment is not clear). • The IDC Distressed Fund was established following the financial crisis to assist companies. "negatively affected by the recessions". A total of ZAR 6 billion was allocated to the fund, with ZAR 1.4 billion distributed in 2009/2010. The uptake of the programme since 2010 is unclear, although the fund remains available to distressed firms. Funding is available in the form of debt at preferential rates or equity. • The Clothing and Textile Production Incentive Programme was introduced in 2010 in order to support and restructure the struggling clothing and textiles sectors through the provision of grants for certain "competitiveness enhancement" expenditures. • The Preferential Procurement Policy Framework Act (PPPFA) first promulgated in 2000, makes provision for preferential procurement (or local content) to be used as a form of industrial policy. Six sectors have thus far been designated as strategic sectors in 2012 to be subject to preferential procurement regulations, with the aim of driving local industrialisation in the respective sectors. These sectors are Power Pylons; Rolling Stock; Buses; Canned Vegetables; Clothing, Textiles, Footwear and Leather products and Set Top Boxes.
South Africa should participate in and fully implement emerging international initiatives to strengthen banking regulation. Particular attention should be paid to addressing the too-big-to-fail problem.	Further steps have been taken towards the implementation of a "twin-peaks" model of financial regulation, with the first draft of legislation currently being prepared and expected to be tabled before parliament in 2013. In addition, Basel 2.5 regulations have been implemented from January 2012, and Basel III regulations have been finalised and are on track to be implemented from 1 January 2013. Solvency 2, and Treat Customer Fairly requirements (a first draft of revised regulations was circulated for comment in March 2012 and a second version is currently being drafted).

Recommendations	Actions taken since the previous *Survey* (July 2010)
Improving framework conditions for business	
Product market regulation should be made less restrictive, particularly as regards barriers to entrepreneurship. Regulation should be simplified and compliance eased. The burden of product market regulation should be lightened and competition policy strengthened.	There have been a number of interventions to encourage the development of new and small businesses over the past two years. These include: ● The new Companies Act, which was implemented on 1 May 2011, has had some impact in reducing product market regulation. Starting a business has become easier (new firms are no longer required to reserve a company name and the number of incorporation documents required have been reduced), business liquidation has been made less restrictive (instead of a company in financial distress going under judicial management, a rescue process can be initiated by the workers and management of a company), and SMME's are no longer required to produce audited financial statements. ● Property transfer was made less costly and more efficient through the introduction of electronic filing for transfer duties by the South African Revenue Service. ● In the 2012 National Budget, the Treasury increased the tax threshold for firms, in order to encourage the growth of small businesses. ● A regulatory framework review process has begun in the mining–sector to make South Africa competitive with regulatory regimes of other competing mining destinations. The Competition Commission continues to investigate anti-competitive behaviour and has made a number of high profile referrals to the Competition Tribunal which has resulted in hefty penalties being handed out to offending firms.
The level and dispersion of import tariffs should be reduced further to encourage competition and long-term productivity growth.	No action.
Raising the saving rate	
A tighter fiscal policy over the cycle should be achieved to raise public saving and contribute to an overall increase in the domestic saving rate.	Successive Budgets and Medium-Term Budget Plan Strategies have affirmed the government's recognition that fiscal consolidation is needed to stabilise and then reduce the ratio of public debt to GDP. It is also recognised that such a consolidation would contribute to the goal of higher national saving.
Pension arrangements should be designed with a view to increasing private saving, in conjunction with other goals. Compulsory pension saving by employees is one promising way of doing this, while positive results might also be achieved via compulsory enrolment with an option to withdraw, particularly in combination with a "save more tomorrow" mechanism.	The Treasury has released a series of draft policy papers in recent months for public comment. The papers make proposals for the reform of the pension industry with the aim of reducing costs, simplifying products, enhancing preservation and broadening the tax incentives on discretionary savings.
Increase the contribution of exports to growth	
Fiscal policy should be made countercyclical with respect to commodity prices and net private capital inflows in order to offset the associated waves of upward pressure on net private capital inflows in order to offset the associated waves of upward pressure on the exchange rate during upswings.	No action.
As long as the level of international reserves remains relatively low and most signs point to overvaluation of the currency, the SARB should allow for a faster accumulation of reserves when private capital inflows are strong and pressure for rand appreciation is high. Intervention in the foreign exchange market should be backed by verbal guidance to the market as to whether the real exchange rate appears to be misaligned.	The SARB increased its holdings of foreign exchange and gold reserves by USD 7.4 billion between July 2010 and April 2011, but there has been little net reserve accumulation since, despite high levels of rand over-valuation for much of 2011 and the first four months of 2012.

Recommendations	Actions taken since the previous *Survey* (July 2010)
Remaining restrictions on capital outflows should be removed and replaced by prudential regulation.	Exchange controls on individuals and institutional investors have been relaxed over the past two years. Relaxations include: • Limits on individuals moving money abroad - previously a ZAR 4 million lifetime investment allowance and a ZAR 750 000 annual discretionary allowance - have been replaced by a ZAR 5 million annual allowance. • Prudential limits on foreign investment by institutional investors have been increased by 5%. • Change in classification of inward listed shares on the Johannesburg Stock Exchange from foreign to domestic (allowing South Africans to trade these shares without limits).

Climate change mitigation

A carbon tax should be introduced.	A carbon tax has yet to be introduced, but a policy paper is currently being drafted by the Treasury for public discussion.
Greater use should be made of other green taxes, such as fuel levies.	The general fuel levy was increased by a total of 30 cents a litre over the past two years, and total fuel taxes by 46 cents a litre.
Electricity prices should be allowed to rise further, in order to fully cover capital costs. Favourable pricing arrangements for large industrial users of electricity should be renegotiated.	The energy regulator NERSA approved electricity tariff increases for Eskom amounting to a cumulative 46% over the past two years. Prices however remain below levels necessary to fully recover costs. Eskom is currently seeking 16% annual tariff increases for each of the next five years. Eskom has been attempting to exit special contracts made with large electricity users. It recently announced that it will be referring its favourable pricing contract with BHP Billiton (which operates highly electricity intensive smelters in the country) to NERSA for review.
Ambitious targets for the development of renewable sources of energy should be established and implemented.	The Department of Energy is in the process of adjudicating bids for the provision of renewable energy as part of its Renewable Energy Independent Power Producers Programme (REIPP). The Department aims to bring 3 725 MW of renewable energy online between 2014 and 2016 through the REIPP. Thus far, the Department has allocated 2 559 MW to preferred bidders over two bid rounds. A third bid round, where the remaining 1 165.6 MW capacity will be allocated will take place in the near future.

Strengthening monetary policy

To further increase transparency and signal commitment to price stability over the longer term, the SARB should consider moving in the direction of announcing a future policy-rate path consistent with the inflation objective. At a first stage, this might involve merely signalling the expected direction of future movements in policy rates.	No action.

Enhancing the stabilising role of fiscal policy and safeguarding fiscal sustainability

South Africa might benefit from mechanisms to prevent a weakening of fiscal discipline in cyclical upswings. These could usefully include a target on the structural balance, buttressed by an expenditure rule.	The government has reiterated its intention to reduce the structural deficit and create the fiscal space to respond to future variations in the business cycle and external shocks. While there is still no formal expenditure rule, the 2013 Medium Term Expenditure Framework Guidelines rule out any increase in spending in 2013/14 and 2014/15 relative to the projections in the 2012 Budget.
In any event, work on assessing the underlying fiscal position should be further developed, and more detailed information about the business cycle and the structural balance should be published.	National Treasury is the process of completing a long-term fiscal report. A summary of main findings will be released in early 2013 with the full report to follow later in the year. The report considers the impact of demographic and economic trends on fiscal sustainability over the coming decades.
Even in the absence of a structural balance target, an expenditure rule element could be introduced by making the broad parameters for the out years set out in the annual Budget and the Medium Term Budget Policy Statement legally binding, such that legal amendments would be required to revise them.	No action.

Recommendations	Actions taken since the previous *Survey* (July 2010)
Consideration should be given to strengthening the link between commodity prices and the fiscal balance; if this link is strengthened, establishment of a commodity fund can be considered to ensure that windfall revenues are saved. In the meantime, such windfalls should be used to reduce debt.	No action.
The government should continue to seek opportunities to increase the efficiency of public expenditure.	A number of government agencies, most notably the Public Protector, have become more assertive in holding public officials accountable for inefficient or corrupt expenditure. The National Treasury continues to develop implementation and monitoring frameworks, together with intervening as required in provincial and local government departments with inadequate administrative capacity.
Wage-setting	
The within-sector legal extension of collective bargaining agreements should be curtailed.	No action.
The level of co-ordination in collective bargaining should be increased to allow for greater influence of outsiders on wages and conditions and to bolster the credibility of the inflation target range.	No action.
Employment regulation	
Enforcement of existing labour laws relating to labour broking should be tightened, but liberal arrangements for temporary employment should be maintained.	The Department of Labour has proposed amendments to key labour laws, some of which are currently being considered by Parliament. In its current form the amendments will address some persisting concerns with labour broking, but it will also tighten the controls on "legitimate" temporary employment services.
The arbitration process for dismissals for cause should be speeded up and simplified.	No action.
Reducing youth unemployment	
Efforts to strengthen job search assistance should be intensified.	No progress thus far, but the Department of Labour plans to embark on a programme of strengthening its labour centres around the country in the 2013/2014 fiscal year.
The use of wage subsidies should be expanded, possibly by building on the existing learnerships, but with a reduced administrative burden.	A policy discussion document on a youth wage subsidy was published by the National Treasury in February 2011. Only limited progress has been made since however, with agreement on policy design yet to be reached at NEDLAC.
Minimum wages should be differentiated by age.	No action.
Probationary requirements in respect of new hires of young employees should be extended.	No action.
Programmes to develop entrepreneurship among the young in disadvantaged groups should be expanded.	No action.
Other	
Improvements in basic education should be prioritised, even though the contribution to raising employment will be small in the near term.	Progress is on-going with respect to the provision of school infrastructure (under the Accelerated Schools Infrastructure Delivery Initiative), distribution of workbooks (under the National Workbook Programme) and expanding early-childhood development (through increased access to pre-school/ Grade R).

Recommendations	Actions taken since the previous *Survey* (July 2010)
Further urbanisation should be facilitated to mitigate spatial mismatches: urban transport should be developed and affordable urban housing expanded.	Some progress has been made in developing urban transport and housing development: ● The Bus Rapid Transit system began operating in Johannesburg and Cape Town in 2009 and 2010 respectively, and the Nelson Mandela Bay area is scheduled to offer a similar service starting in 2013. A further ten cities are either finalising public transport plans or building public transport networks. The national government has allocated ZAR 16.4 billion between 2012/13 and 2014/15 towards the construction of these networks. The Passenger Rail Agency of South Africa (PRASA) is currently in the process of replacing Metrorail's aging rail-car stock, a process that will continue over the next twenty years and for which government has allocated ZAR 40 billion. Government is also contributing funds towards the replacement of PRASA's dated rail signalling systems. In the 2012 budget, ZAR 50.5 billion was allocated to low-income housing and the upgrading of informal settlements in secondary cities as well as ZAR 27 billion for upgrading informal settlements in large cities over the next 3 years. ● Government continues to support urban housing development. Capital subsidies are available to developers of medium-density rental housing projects in designated areas, and tax incentives are on offer for rental apartment building upgrades and conversions in the inner city. Finance-linked subsidies are also available to households in the affordable housing market. ● Government, under the National Upgrading Support Programme, continues to assist in the upgrading of informal settlements by co-ordinating activity amongst various stakeholders and across the different spheres of government, as well providing technical support to municipalities on infrastructure improvement projects. ● The Infrastructure Skills Grant provides funding to train interns in engineering and spatial planning and since 2011/12, the grant has paid for 150 graduates in six large municipalities and water boards. Over the medium term, funding will be provided to train a further 1 000 graduates.
Access to credit for business start-ups should be improved, for example by easing collateral constraints.	Khula, SAMAF (South African Microfinance Apex Fund) and the IDC's small business lending portfolio were merged in 2012 to create the Small Enterprise Finance Agency (SEFA) which will act as a subsidiary of the IDC. The move was aimed at consolidating the fragmented small business lending space and reducing the reliance on financial intermediaries which have been hesitant to lend post-crisis. SEFA will be able to leverage off of the IDC's strong risk and balance sheet management expertise, and thus make loans directly to businesses. SEFA will continue to provide wholesale loans to financial intermediaries but will also lend directly to businesses and provide credit guarantees for businesses requiring bank finance. Loans of up to ZAR 3 million will be granted.

Chapter 1

Improving education quality in South Africa

South Africa has achieved remarkable progress in educational attainment relative to other emerging countries, but the quality of basic education for a large fraction of the Black African population is still very low. This chapter identifies several hurdles to the upgrading of basic education quality, such as the lack of investment in school infrastructure and learning materials in disadvantaged areas, uneven administrative capacity at the local level, low teacher quality and poor teaching of English among Black Africans. Bold action is recommended to empower schools with more physical resources, more competent school leadership and an accountable teacher workforce. Skill mismatches of supply and demand on the labour market may be further addressed by vocational education reforms and an alleviation of credit constraints at the tertiary level.

The statistical data for Israel are supplied by and under the responsibility of the relevant Israeli authorities. The use of such data by the OECD is without prejudice to the status of the Golan Heights, East Jerusalem and Israeli settlements in the West Bank under the terms of international law.

South Africa has reached high educational attainment but quality of education remains dismal

South Africa has reached high educational attainment relative to other emerging countries, but education quality has been low and very uneven. There appear to be large returns to education at the upper secondary and tertiary levels and a significant payoff to education quality in the labour market, suggesting that there would be high economic returns to increasing the supply of high-school graduates with good passing marks who are able to go on to tertiary education.

Towards universal attainment in primary and secondary schools

Educational attainment has reached high levels relative to emerging economies

Sustained educational progress has taken place in recent decades, including the last years of the apartheid era and continuing since the advent of democracy. As a result, 89% of the population aged over 15 years was literate in 2004, a proportion that reaches 98% among the 15-24 year old population. As shown in Figure 1.1, average years of schooling attained by young adults aged 25-29 year old have increased by about one year every decade since 1960, which is reasonably fast by international standards. Between 1960 and 2010, young South Africans have closed about half of the gap in years of schooling relative to young Americans, but no convergence with respect to the world educational attainment leader (Korea) has been observed over the last twenty years. Today, South African young adults spend more years at school than their counterparts from other emerging economies such as China or India. Mean educational attainment of the young adults cohort is about the same as in Brazil.

Figure 1.1. **Mean years of schooling**
Mean years of schooling of population 25-29

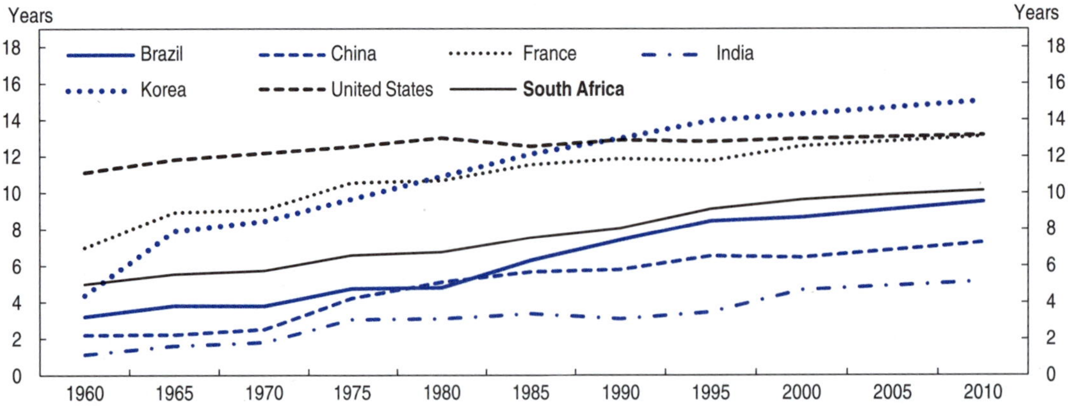

Source: South Africa data is based on *Community Survey* (Statistics South Africa, 2007) and calculations made by Louw, van der Berg and Yu (2006). Population aged 25-29 is proxied by population aged 27. Other countries are drawn from OECD (2012a) long-term projections.

StatLink ⟲ *http://dx.doi.org/10.1787/888932783154*

The increase in educational attainment has nevertheless slowed down recently. While the annual change in mean years of schooling among young adults was 0.10 over the 1960-2010 period, it was only 0.04 between 2005 and 2010. Over the same period, annual changes in mean years of schooling have been larger in other emerging economies such as Brazil, China or India, and also among more developed countries like France or Korea, such that South Africa is no longer clearly converging towards advanced country levels of years of schooling. Hence South Africa would need to restart the education engine to maintain its leadership among major emerging countries in terms of educational attainment.

School attendance in South Africa

The relatively high level of educational attainment in South Africa is largely attributable to near full enrolment in primary and secondary education, with corresponding gross enrolment rates of 102% and 94% in 2009 (World Bank, 2012).[1] This performance is in line with the South African Schools Act of 1996, which made schooling mandatory from age 7 until 15 or grade 9 (Box 1.1).

Box 1.1. The South African education system

Education for black South Africans during the apartheid regime was under central government control, which reinforced racial and geographical segregation. Enrolment increased but infrastructure was largely inadequate, pupil-teacher ratios were huge and the curriculum was biased and openly racist. In 1986 spending per pupil was nine times higher for white learners than for Black Africans (OECD, 2008).

Since 1994 the government has profoundly reshaped the education system, which has been broken down into nine provincial sub-systems. Education financing has been redirected to take into consideration equity and affordability issues. School governance has been decentralised, with greater autonomy devolved to school governing bodies, which among other things received the right to charge fees. The curriculum has been reviewed several times.

Education is compulsory in South Africa from age seven (grade 1) to age 15 or the completion of grade 9 and enrolment in these grades is almost universal. Between grades 10 through 12 learners can choose between a vocational training route in a Further Education and Training college or to continue their education in the basic education system. Those who choose the vocational route complete it with a National Certificate Vocational (NCV). The nationally administered National Senior Certificate (NSC) taken in grade 12 represents the completion of basic education and continues to be the preferred choice. Enrolment rates are high, but levels of grade repetition are also high, especially in grades 10 and 11, and the majority of learners (58%) still leave the schooling system without completing a national leaving certificate (NCV or NSC) commonly known as matric.

Over the last decade, substantial progress in attendance rates at educational institutions have been recorded for children below age 7. As shown in Figure 1.2, the share of children aged 5 attending an educational institution doubled between 2002 and 2009. Similarly, early childhood education (below age 5) is expanding rapidly and reached 64% of children aged 3-5 years in 2010 (Department of Basic Education, 2012) thanks to the

Figure 1.2. **Attendance rates**

Share of population attending an educational institution by age group

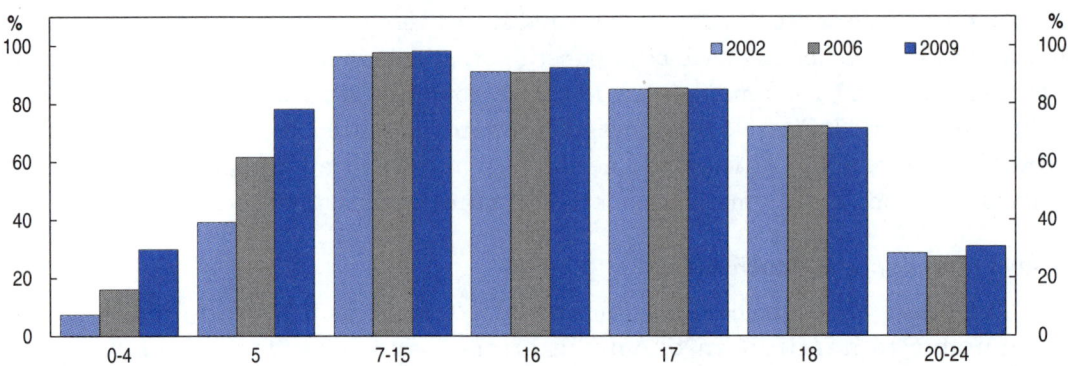

Source: Education for All, Department of Basic Education, 2010a.

StatLink ᴴᴵˢᴾ http://dx.doi.org/10.1787/888932783173

considerable efforts made recently by the government to increase the number of early education facilities.

As with early childhood education, tertiary education has been growing, whereas the diffusion of education at the upper secondary level has come to a standstill over the last decade. At age 18, 71.5% of youth attended an educational institution in 2009, the same percentage as in 2002. The proportion of cohorts aged 16-18 years attending upper secondary has not varied since 2002 (83% according to Department of Basic Education, 2011a). Enrolment in higher education has increased at a 5% annual rate since 2000, but reached only 840 000 students in 2011 or 18% of the 18-24 years population (about the same level as in Brazil, a country with comparable income and similarly high income inequality). When all educational institutions are considered (including vocational schools), the enrolment rate of the 20-24 years age group reaches 30%, a slightly higher percentage than in 2002.

Educational attainment remains polarised but the gap has narrowed

Almost twenty years after the end of apartheid, the education gap between Black Africans and Whites has narrowed as shown by Figure 1.3, which splits mean educational attainment by race as calculated by Louw, van der Berg and Yu (2006).

Yet, education outcomes still differ a lot across race. For instance, the pass rate in 2009 in the National Senior Certificate examination, which corresponds to grade 12 in the general education system, was equal to 57% among African, 80% among Coloured, 89% among Indian/Asian and 99% among White, with an average of 62% across all pupils.

Educational attainment and matric pass rates are also unevenly distributed across regions with higher rates in more urbanised areas. While the percentage of children aged 7-15 attending compulsory basic education is broadly the same across regions, gross enrolment rates in secondary schooling vary widely. Moreover, attendance rates are often inversely related to the pass rate at the matric (Department of Basic Education, 2010a).

In contrast, South Africa has broadly achieved gender parity in school enrolment. This is a remarkable achievement given that gender parity is not observed in other emerging countries like India or Brazil.

Figure 1.3. **Mean years of schooling by ethnic group**

Mean years of schooling at age 27

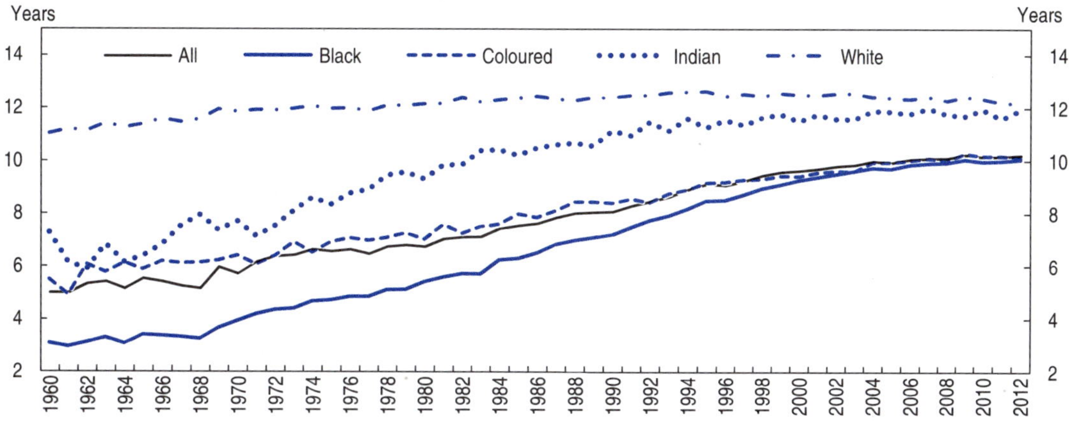

Source: South Africa data is based on *Community Survey* (Statistics South Africa, 2007) and calculations made by Louw, van der Berg and Yu (2006).

StatLink ᵐˢ᪲ *http://dx.doi.org/10.1787/888932783192*

Basic education displays low quality and high inequality

There is much evidence, from both international and national surveys, that education quality remains poor overall and uneven across regions and population groups, which largely reflects the country's historical legacy.

Evidence from international surveys

The rankings of South Africa in international tests of pupils' competencies in reading (PIRLS, 2006) and mathematics (TIMSS, 2003, Reddy, 2006) have been dismal. Countries with lower income such as Indonesia or Egypt have performed better in the latter surveys, with South Africa displaying the worst average test scores among the sample of countries (Figure 1.4). The most recent evidence (TIMSS, 2011, Human Sciences Research Council, 2012) shows a marked improvement in average test scores, but South Africa still ranks at the bottom of the international spectrum. Other regional surveys of education performance display comparable results. With a GDP per capita less than one fifth as large, Kenya performed significantly better than South Africa in SACMEQ (2007) reading and mathematics tests in 2000 and 2007. Moreover, there was no improvement in SACMEQ tests between 2000 and 2007. These findings underline the need for urgent and sustained intervention. Importantly, the experience gained at the international level could be better brought to bear in South Africa if it decided to join the Programme for International Student Assessment (PISA) and the Teaching and Learning International Survey (TALIS), and to undertake an *OECD Review of Evaluation and Assessment in Education* like Mexico recently (OECD, 2012b).

South Africa's poor performance in terms of average scores in international tests and regional surveys is explained by the large fraction of students who do not reach basic qualification standards, while the top quintile of students perform reasonably well. As a result, inequality in test scores is among the highest observed in the sample (see Figure 1.4). Improving the performance of students at the bottom of the test score distribution therefore constitutes the best strategy to improve average results and simultaneously reduce inequality in educational outcomes.

Figure 1.4. **International tests of scholastic achievement**

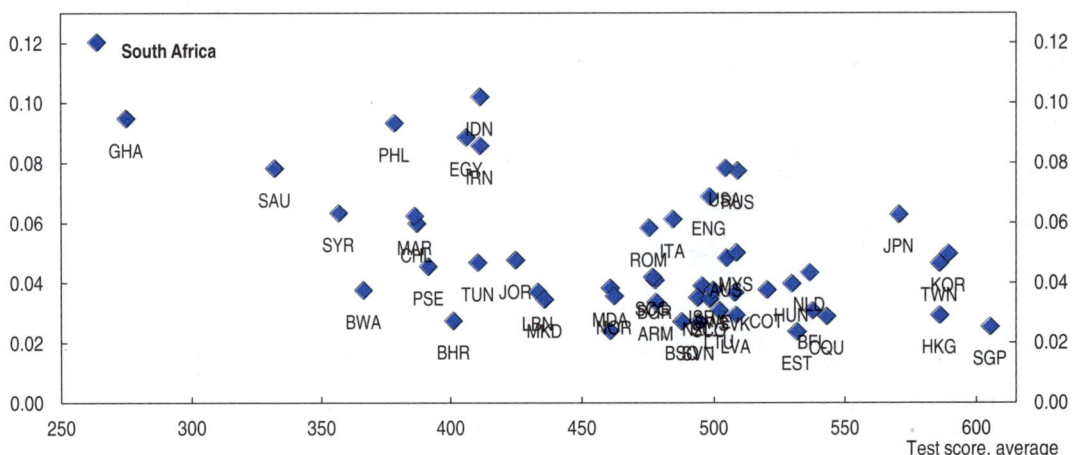

A. Mathematics Achievement (TIMSS 2003)

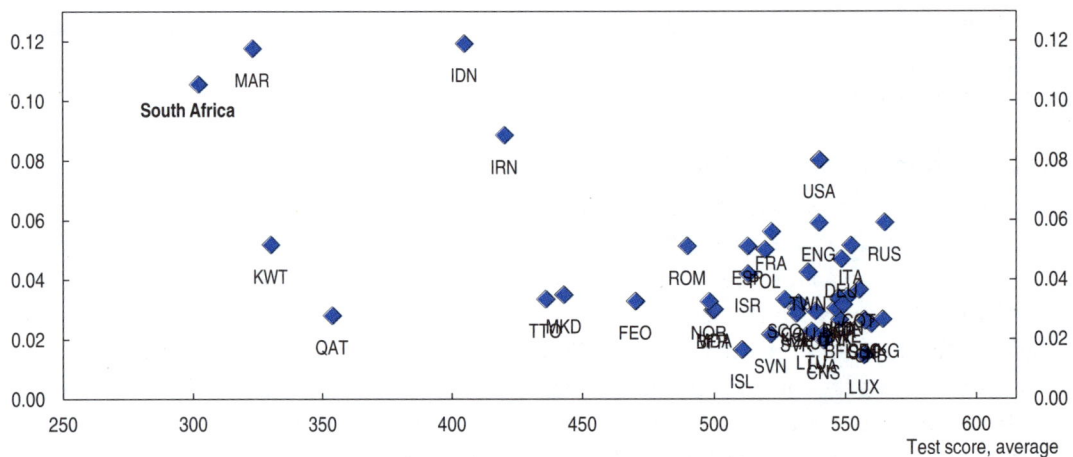

B. Reading Achievement (PIRLS 2006)

Source: TIMSS (2003), PIRLS (2006) and OECD calculations.

StatLink http://dx.doi.org/10.1787/888932783211

National evidence

At the national level, several indicators such as net enrolment and repetition rates point to quality issues in the education system. For instance, the net enrolment rate in primary education has been falling since 1995 and was substantially lower (85% in 2009 according to World Bank, 2012) than the gross enrolment rate, a gap explained by a high repetition rate (10.3% in 2010 according to Department of Basic Education, 2012). The repetition rate in primary education fell significantly over the 1997-2005 period, but then picked up again. Repeating a grade occurs at a higher frequency rate in grade 1 (13.1%) and in years that precede the matric examination (24.4% and 24.3% in grades 10 and 11), an outcome likely explained by schools aiming to improve their matric pass rate.

There is still a substantial fraction of children left out of school, although there is conflicting evidence on this issue. On the one hand, the World Bank (2012) reports that the proportion of children of primary school age being out-of-school has increased over time, but on the other hand, the share of out-of-school children among the cohort aged 7-15 years fell between 2002 and 2009 (Department of Basic Education, 2010a, Table 7, p. 21). One hypothesis that would reconcile these two views is that an increasing proportion of children join school with some years of delay, but that fewer children never go to school.

Private returns to educational investments are large

This section describes original evidence on the level and trend of private returns to schooling. Private returns to schooling are shown to be high, especially at the tertiary level. Moreover, education quality appears to have a direct monetary reward on the labour market irrespective of any return for higher educational attainment.

Returns to schooling

In-depth analysis of the wage and employability premiums associated with different educational levels among Black Africans and at the national level between 1994 and 2010, is presented in Branson and Leibbrandt (2013a), which was commissioned for this *Economic Survey*, and summarised in Annex 1.A1. There are large differences in the size and trend of the wage premiums associated with different levels of education relative to the population that has received only primary education, which is mostly composed of Black Africans. Both the earnings and employment probability premiums to tertiary are very high (the Mincer return to tertiary schooling is around 18% while international estimates generally range between 6 and 14%) and have increased over the period. As shown in Figure 1.5, incomplete secondary and matric earnings premiums are respectively close to 6 and 11%, and they have remained constant over the period. These patterns suggest increasing returns to schooling as in several other emerging economies (see Colclough *et al.*, 2010).

Returns to education are significantly lower for Black Africans relative to the national average, which may be linked to differences in school quality and persistent discrimination. The wage premium is lower for African males at any educational level but above all for those with a matric (Figure 1.5).

Figure 1.5. **Returns to schooling, 2010 – Males**

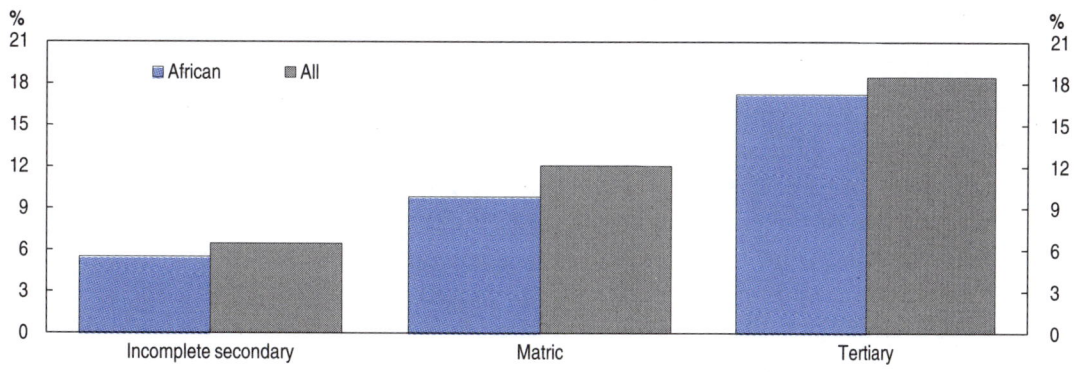

Source: Branson and Leibbrandt (2013a).

StatLink ᴍ︎ᴤ︎ᴸ︎ *http://dx.doi.org/10.1787/888932783230*

Labour market returns to school quality

Levelling out standards in school quality can have large impacts on an individual's prospects on the labour market. First, school quality can affect educational achievement. Case and Deaton (1999) find that decreasing the pupil/teacher ratio by 10 children improves average educational attainment by 0.6 years. Second, school quality, even controlling for education level, may affect workers' productivity and their ability to find or maintain a job.

The labour market returns in terms of wage and employability premiums of school quality are investigated in Branson and Leibbrandt (2013b), which was commissioned for this *Economic Survey*, and briefly described in Annex 1.A2. The authors merge income and employment panel data (National Income Dynamics Study) with historical education data from the Department of Basic Education. The sample is composed of prime working-age African adults (aged 32-59 years in 2008) who have completed their education before the end of apartheid. As the mobility of Black Africans was largely restricted at that time, this population group was exposed in an exogenous way to different levels of school quality, which varied substantially across communities. Variables are constructed to proxy the degree of school quality observed in the respondent's school. As the latter is not observed, the authors select the pupil-teacher ratio of the high school closest to the place of living of the respondent. Branson *et al.* (2012) find that over 70% of South African learners in 2008 attend either their closest school or a school within 2 km of their closest school. Finally, when regressing log earnings on pupil-teacher ratio, educational attainment and age, the authors also control for a large set of additional variables such as marital status, parental education, urban residence and a full set of dummies for the district council of birth capturing unmeasured characteristics at the district level.

The pupil-teacher ratio is found to have a direct and large positive effect on the earnings of Black African males. On average, decreasing the pupil/teacher ratio by one learner is associated with about one percent increase in earnings. Moreover, the relationship between earnings and school quality appears to be stronger among those with only primary education. One possible reason is that, in a good quality school, those leaving with primary education still manage to achieve a basic degree of literacy and numeracy, while those in poor-quality schools are illiterate and or innumerate.

No robust relationship was found with employment. The less apparent relationship between employment and school quality and its strong association with earnings could signal that the difference in school quality is differentiating workers' skills in ways that are not immediately evident to an employer, but materialise once the individual is employed.

The magnitude of the estimated effect of the pupil-teacher ratio on earnings is further illustrated on Figure 1.6. The earnings premium paid to school quality is calculated for different quantiles of the current distribution of pupil-teacher ratio, and by location (the data were extracted from the Department of Basic Education, 2009a, *Systemic study at grade* 9). The results represent the relative wage gap among adults that is associated with differences in school quality. It turns out that studying in a school in the bottom decile (*i.e.* with a pupil-teacher ratio below 20) would imply at least a 10% wage gain relative to future earnings of a pupil attending a school with a median pupil-teacher ratio (*i.e.* 28.1 in this database). Similarly, attending a school in the upper decile (*i.e.* with ratios above 35.7) is associated with at least a 10% wage penalty.

Figure 1.6. **Labour market outcome of schooling quality**

Relative wage variation due to differences in the pupil-teacher ratio

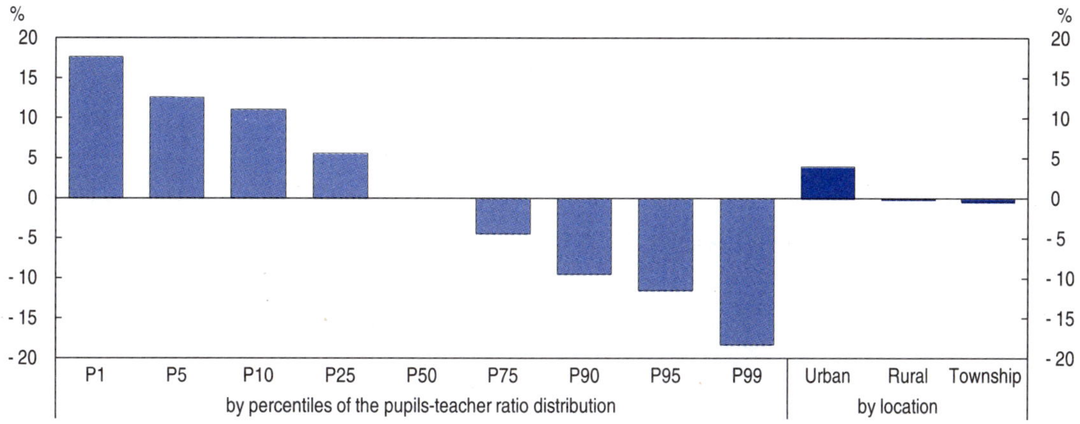

Source: Branson and Leibbrandt (2013b) and OECD calculations.

StatLink ᴬˢᴾ http://dx.doi.org/10.1787/888932783249

Improving education quality

Education quality, as measured for instance by students' average performance in test scores, depends on the amount of resources injected into the education system as well as on institutional settings that condition the efficient use of available resources. Both aspects are reviewed in this section. The adequacy of school outcomes to meet labour market needs is discussed in a third part.

The education system is short of physical and human resources

In the following section, the budget of the basic education system is evaluated against international standards. There is evidence of physical and human resource shortages, as well as an unequal distribution of available resources.

Basic education is lacking resources

In 2010, public expenditure on educational institutions and administration represented 5.9% of GDP. About 2.5% of GDP were spent on primary education, 2.0% on secondary, 0.64% on tertiary, and 0.06% on pre-primary. Expenditure as a share of GDP was slightly higher than in Mexico and about the same as in Brazil or an average OECD country (World Bank, 2012). These figures are often quoted to make the point that there is no apparent under-funding of the education system. However, this view is inaccurate as the proportion of the population aged 0-14 years in South Africa (29.9% in 2011) is much higher than in OECD countries (e.g. 18.4% in France and 20.1% in the United States). This share is somewhat higher than even some other emerging countries, such as Brazil (25.0%). Even more strikingly, half of the South African population is less than 24 years old, many of whom should be attending an educational institution.

Public resources spent per pupil would need to be increased by 30% at the primary level and by 20% at the secondary level to match the OECD average level of resources per pupil. In this calculation, public spending per pupil is expressed as a share of GDP per capita, a proxy for cross-country differences in income. As shown on Figure 1.7, resource intensity has increased slightly in South African primary schools since 2003, but it has stagnated in secondary schools. This observation does not conflict with the fact that

Figure 1.7. **Primary and secondary resources**

Public expenditure per pupil (% GDP per capita)

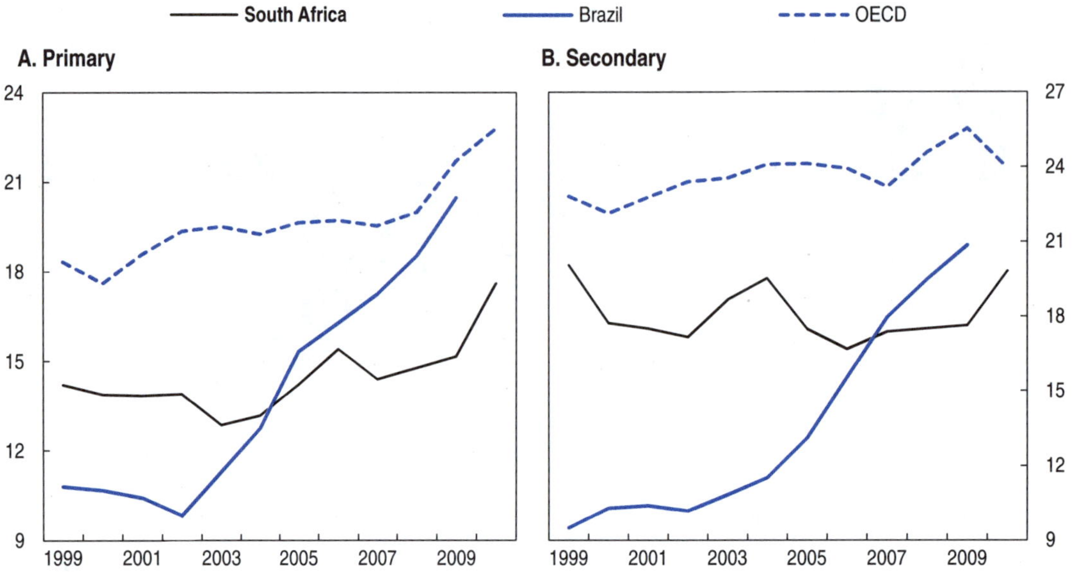

Source: World Bank (2012).

StatLink ᴍᴀᴘ http://dx.doi.org/10.1787/888932783268

expenditure per student has substantially increased since the end of apartheid, but underlines a stagnation relative to productivity and wage gains realised over the period.

The gap in per capita learner expenditure across provinces has been reduced over the last decade. In 2007 expenditures per learner ranged between ZAR 5 029 in Limpopo and ZAR 7 381 in Free State, with a national average at ZAR 5 787 (OECD, 2008). In part this trend is due to a significant improvement in funding equity both between provinces and schools thanks to the implementation of redistributive policies (see below).

The most pressing problems perceived by students concern, in order of priority, the lack of books, high fees, large class sizes, poor teaching and teacher absenteeism (Statistics South Africa, 2011, Table 4). These issues have been repeatedly emphasised in the past. Lack of books and large classes are more common in the province of North West, while high school fees have mostly concerned Gauteng, Western Cape and Mpumalanga. On the other hand, teachers generally point to perceived lower wages and poor benefits, work overload and disintegration of student discipline (OECD, 2008).

The government has made several sets of recommendations to address these weaknesses (Box 1.2). While the most pressing concerns have been well identified, thanks to an impressive collection of data in the form of surveys and analysis conducted by administrative federal authorities over recent years, increases in allocated budgets have not always materialised on the ground, according to the Action Plan to 2014 (Department of Basic Education, 2011b), due to a lack of administrative capacity at the local level.

Upgrade existing school infrastructure and equipment

Although some progress has been made, many schools from disadvantaged areas still suffer from important infrastructure backlogs, which have largely been inherited from the apartheid era. Thanks to a proper registration of needs and current backlogs through the

> ## Box 1.2. **Key priorities identified in the National Development Plan, the Action Plan to 2014 and the New Growth Path**
>
> **The National Development Plan (National Planning Commission, 2012) makes the following recommendations to improve the education system:**
>
> - Achieve high-quality early education with an emphasis on child nutrition. Every child should receive at least two years of pre-school education.
>
> - Improve education quality by upgrading the management of the system, with supportive and corrective measures targeting low-performing schools, and an infrastructure campaign in poor schools especially in rural areas. Improve the competence and capacity of school principals, emphasising a higher degree of selection among applicants, greater management powers and greater accountability.
>
> - Improve teacher accountability. Issues related to teacher performance such as training, remuneration, incentives, teaching time and performance measurement are discussed.
>
> - Expand the size and quality of the further education and training system, by improving the relevance of the curriculum.
>
> - Increase participation and graduation rates at university for Black students and enhance R&D at university and in the private sector.
>
> **The Action Plan to 2014 (Department of Basic Education, 2011b) has the following 5 priority goals:**
>
> - Improve the access of children to quality Early Childhood Development (ECD) below grade 1.
>
> - Improve the professionalism, teaching skills, subject knowledge and computer literacy of teachers throughout their entire career.
>
> - Ensure that every learner has access to the minimum set of textbooks and workbooks required according to national policy standards.
>
> - Ensure that the basic annual management processes take place across all schools in the country in a way that contributes towards a functional school environment.
>
> - Improve the frequency and quality of the monitoring and support services provided to schools by district offices, partly through better use of e-Education.
>
> **The New Growth Path (The Economic Development Department, 2010) has several quantitative objectives:**
>
> - Engineers and artisans: Target 30 000 additional engineers and 50 000 additional artisans by 2014-15.
>
> - Workplace skills (SETA): Improve skills in every job and target 1.2 million workers for certified on-the-job skills improvement programmes annually from 2013.
>
> - Further education and training (FET): Expand enrolment at FET colleges, targeting a million students in FET colleges by 2014 up from 420 000 in 2008, and increase graduation rates.

National Education Infrastructure Management (NEIMS), the number of schools without water or without toilets has been divided by 5 between 1996 and 2010 (Action Plan to 2014, Department of Basic Education, 2011b, p. 152), and the proposition of overcrowed classes (over 45 learners) declined from 55% to 25%. Yet, provision of school infrastructure remains a serious challenge as for instance 77% had no computer centre, 60% had no library in 2010, 7% still had no water supply, and overall 23% were deemed to be in poor or very poor condition, among which two thirds were located in Eastern Cape and KwaZulu-Natal (Department of Basic Education, 2011b, p. 150, from *NEIMS Database*).

In 2009, the government implemented the Accelerated Schools Infrastructure Delivery Initiative (ASIDI), which is aimed at upgrading infrastructure and increasing the availability of learning materials in targeted schools, such as schools without water, sanitation, electricity, fencing, schools with deficient construction and overcrowded schools. The projected cost of replacing all inappropriate infrastructures is estimated at ZAR 6 billion (*i.e.* 0.2% of GDP), of which 90% is disproportionately allocated to schools in the Eastern Cape.

The persistent shortage of textbooks illustrates the practical problems faced by the South African government. Statistics from SACMEQ (2007) database show that only 36% of learners had access to their own mathematics textbook. The low textbook availability is the main reason why learners are not allowed to take them home. In Limpopo, 22% of schools that ordered textbooks received nothing in 2008 (Department of Basic Education, 2011b, p. 125), which mainly reflects delivery failures of local authorities. There seem to be fewer problems when procurements are made to schools for purchasing learning materials directly, while using funds from the department (Department of Basic Education, 2010b).

Several ICT initiatives, sometimes involving private companies, have been proposed in various strategic documents, as e-Education is recognised to be an important aspect of the modern economy with which learners need to be familiarised. Yet, backlogs are enormous in rural areas and cross-province disparities in ICT penetration at school are likely to be persistent. Indeed, while wealthy provinces such as Gauteng and Western Cape display excellent coverage, most provinces, especially the Eastern Cape, Limpopo and KwaZulu-Natal, are still lagging far behind (*e.g.* 60% of schools have a computer centre in Western Cape versus only 10% in Eastern Cape).

The South African government has rightly sought to address school equipment problems, which appear to be crucial hurdles in raising education quality. For instance, Case and Deaton (1999) found a positive return to secondary school libraries when estimating outcomes. Oosthuizen and Bhorat (2006) show that schools performing in the upper deciles have greater access to facilities (*i.e.* book rooms, principal's office, copy rooms) as well as greater relative access to equipment, especially overhead projectors and desks. Bhorat and Oosthuizen (2008) echo these findings, especially with regard to desks (per learner) and other equipment such as photocopiers, libraries, and computers.

Evidence suggests a large and robust correlation between ICT and library availability and grade 9 pupils' performance in "Systemic Studies" language test scores in 2009 (Annex 1.A3). Moreover, a very large number of other potential determinants (about 100) are included in the analysis in order to minimise the risk of any omitted variable bias. In this study, the set of explanatory variables includes learner characteristics (race, family wealth and socio-economic background, language spoken at home), school characteristics (physical and human resources, school climate, school principal characteristics), teacher characteristics and teaching policy (teaching intensity, assessment policy) as well as geographical controls.

In this analysis, learning-oriented school equipment stands out as a key lever for improving school outcomes. As expected, contextual variables such as the frequent use of language of test at home (*i.e.* Afrikaans or English), family wealth and some provincial dummies capturing unobserved province-specific characteristics (*i.e.* Free State having a large positive impact, and Limpopo a large negative one), display the largest effects. However, there are also large and robust correlations between test scores and policy variables such as ICT penetration or library availability at schools. For instance, the addition of library and ICT effects is commensurate with the effect associated with contextual variables such as the frequent use of the language of test at home or the constructed index of school historical and socio-economic background, a weighted average derived from a Principal Component Analysis of variables such as the historical classification of schools, the amount of school fees, the quintile classification and school principal's assessment of pupils's socio-economic background.

Figure 1.8 provides a simple illustration of the relationship between reading test scores at grade 9 and a school equipment index, which is the weighted average of school infrastructure (materials used for walls, availability of running water, electricity and toilets), and use of libraries and ICT penetration. It is evident that test scores in the lowest-performing schools are half those in best-performing schools in proportion to the constructed school equipment index, with a marked increase in test scores among the top 10% schools in terms of school equipment.

Figure 1.8. **Language scores**
Average language score by quantiles of the school equipment use index

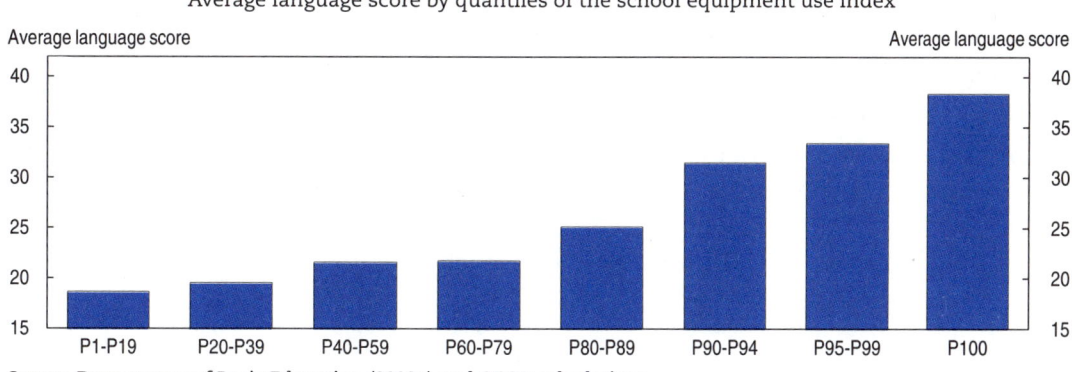

Source: Department of Basic Education (2009a) and OECD calculations.
StatLink http://dx.doi.org/10.1787/888932783287

With these analyses in mind, it is strongly recommended that the South African government pursues and accelerates reforms to upgrade school infrastructure and equipment, while targeting basic school infrastructure (water, electricity), and learning materials (textbooks, libraries and access to ICT). While upgrading basic school infrastructure does not seem to have a significant impact per se (as already noted in several economic studies such as Crouch and Vinjevold, 2006), it is an essential first step before the introduction of additional equipment with stronger value-added such as libraries or ICT. To this end, the share of capital expenditure in total expenditure on public institutions should continue to rise: it increased from 1.1% in 2003 to 4.0% in 2009, but OECD countries spent on average 9.0% on capital at the same date, while Korea, the PISA leader, spent 16.8%.

Increase the quality and number of teachers

There is a severe shortage of good teachers in South Africa. Teachers' knowledge of the subjects they teach has been questioned in both regional tests (SACMEQ, 2007) and national surveys (Taylor et al., 2012). Moreover, South Africa is confronted with a marked teacher shortage. The World Bank (2012) reports a pupil-teacher ratio of 30.7 in primary schools and 25 in secondary schools, almost twice the average level observed in OECD countries (among high-income OECD countries, the pupil-teacher ratio in primary ranges between 9.3 in Sweden and 22.0 in Korea, a country where teachers receive high wages and are deemed to be highly qualified, OECD, 2012d). While some progress has been made at secondary level, the ratio has stagnated in primary schools since the mid-2000s. Moreover, teachers are very unevenly distributed across types of schools. The Department of Basic Education (2011a) reports an average class size of 22 in independent schools, and 36 in public schools. The situation was even worse in FET Colleges and public higher education, where the pupil-teacher ratio was 58.9 and 48.2 in 2005 (OECD, 2008), although some adjustment may be needed for the smaller number of hours taught. In 2009, the share of schools where average class size (which is always larger than the pupil-teacher ratio as some educators registered as teachers do not actually teach) was above 40 learners reached 48% in Mpumalanga, 46% in Limpopo and 44% in KwaZulu-Natal. In comparison, average class size among OECD countries is 21 in primary schools and 23 in secondary schools (OECD, 2012c).

The lack of strong teachers is primarily a long-lasting consequence of the historical context, which has not been addressed successfully by the reform of teacher education. Each year, the number of teacher graduates is around 6 000, well below the replacement needs of approximatively 20 000. This critical situation is aggravated by the fact that about one fourth of newly qualified teachers, especially white teachers, plan to leave the country to teach abroad, and about half of new teachers have recently considered leaving the profession (OECD, 2008).

Among OECD countries, average class size is generally sufficiently low to be considered as a second-order issue. While teachers are usually available in sufficient

Figure 1.9. **Pupil-teacher ratio**

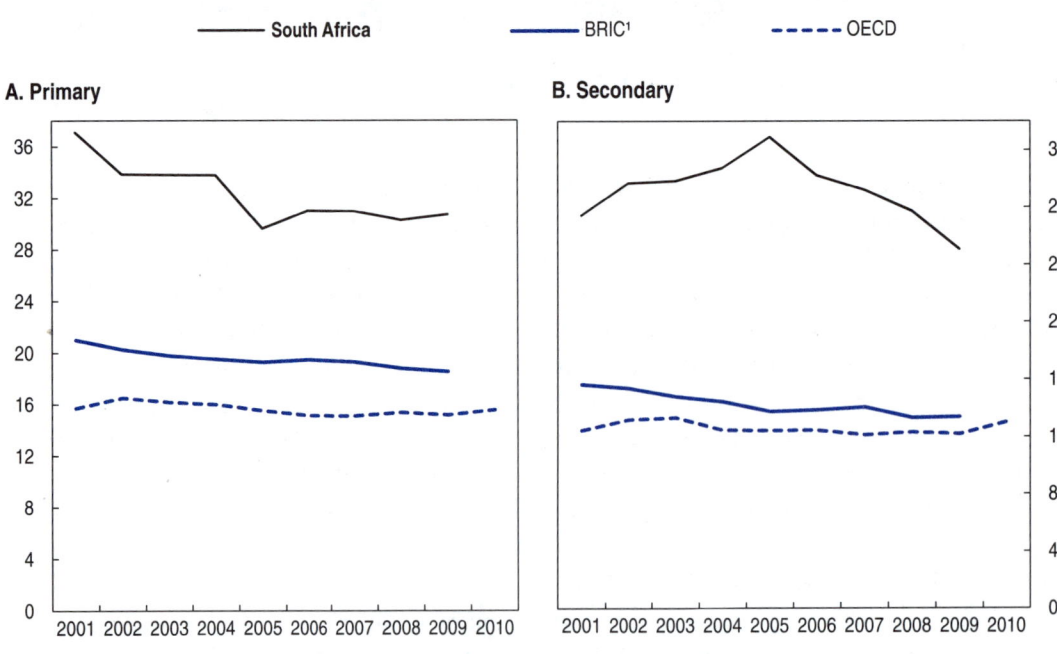

1. Brazil, Russian Federation, Indonesia and China.
Source: World Bank (2012).

StatLink ⧉ *http://dx.doi.org/10.1787/888932783306*

quantity, upgrading teacher quality is a key policy objective recommended by the OECD (2012c). South Africa is facing both teacher quantity and quality issues, which both need to be addressed. As a first step, remedying excessively large class size would be conducive to improvements in education quality. In the context of South Africa, a large number of studies has pointed at teaching dysfunctions in the context of excess class sizes (*e.g.* Crouch and Mabogoane, 2001; Simkins and Paterson, 2005; van der Berg, 2006; De Lannoy and Hall, 2012), a finding partly confirmed by the empirical analysis of Annex 1.A3.

Alongside other issues such as teacher quality and absenteeism, which are addressed below, the South African government has rightly sought to address the teacher shortage problem. For instance, it put in place wage incentives representing as much as 10% of a starting salary in 2007 to attract teachers in rural and remote areas, and also implemented in 2007 the *Funza Lushaka* Bursary programme (see *www.funzalushaka.doe.gov.za* for details) to encourage students entering into the teaching profession. The bursary scheme covers all student expenses, including tuition, accommodation, meals and books and offers a small living allowance. The bursary is to be repaid if recipients fail to graduate or do not take up a post in a public school. This scheme has been very popular and has expanded rapidly. In 2010, about 9 200 bursaries were awarded and about 2 000 graduates were available for placement (Department of Basic Education, 2010a).

Such initiatives should be considerably strengthened to reduce the average class size in basic education, in particular in schools with a clearly identified lack of good teachers. First, the flight of the best teachers abroad should be contained by the provision of adequate incentives and career prospects. Moreover, South Africa may benefit from its relatively higher prosperity to benefit from an increasingly integrated teacher job market, by hiring Indian or African (*e.g.* from Lesotho, Zimbabwe, Zambia) teachers (SACE, 2011). Finally and most importantly, the expansion of the *Funza Lushaka* Bursary programme, which is planned to grow by 30% in 2013, should be fostered. This programme is deemed to be successful as it has led to the training of good quality new teachers. Further expanding this programme could cover a growing part of the annual replacement need for teachers (about 20 000).

Although the South African government is encouraged to go beyond targeting replacement needs, just maintaining the number of teachers would halve the gap in the pupil-teacher ratio in primary with respect to OECD countries by 2030 as the school-age population falls (Figure 1.10).

Figure 1.10. **Projected pupil-teacher ratio**

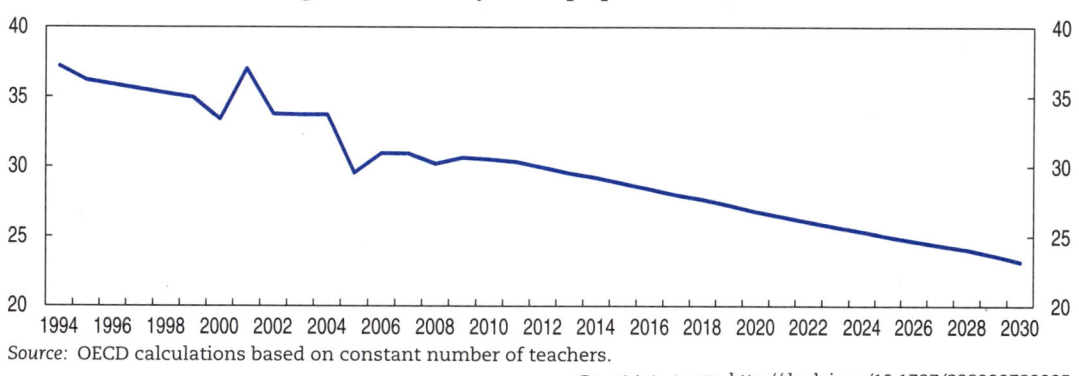

Source: OECD calculations based on constant number of teachers.

StatLink ⟨⟩ http://dx.doi.org/10.1787/888932783325

Make the distribution of school resources more equitable

Inequality in school performance in South Africa has been largely driven by the socio-economic differences in parental background. Social Economic Status (SES) of parents is correlated with child test scores in all PISA countries, but the relationship appears to be stronger in South Africa. While parental SES explains about 13% of the variance in PISA test scores, it explains 20% in the *Systemic Study* analysed in Annex 1.A3, and 22% when an index of school (rather than pupil) socio-economic composition is considered.

The impact of pupils SES on test scores is mitigated by redistributive policies such as National Norms and Standards for School Funding (NNSSF),[2] but it is amplified by the possibility given to School Governing Bodies to charge school fees. The NNSSF framework yielded a classification of schools according to national quintiles based on income, dependency ratio, the unemployment rate and the level of education of the community in the area around a given school. Funding for non-personnel expenditures are allocated such that the poorest quintile receives 30% of the total school allocation and the upper quintile only 5%. The school classification into quintiles and the associated public funding are determined by the average wealth of relatively large communities, and there remain stark differences in school funding within the same community as many schools are allowed to charge fees.

In other words, the current quintile classification of schools is inaccurate as it is based on crude geographical criteria, and it should be replaced by a different and fairer classification based for instance on the median learner's SES within each school (or possibly on any other quantile SES, depending on social preferences). To illustrate this point, an index of learners' parental SES has been constructed from the learner questionnaire of the *Systemic Study* as a weighted average (derived from Principal Component Analysis) of the following household characteristics: household size, orphan dummy, education of mother and father, reading frequency at home, books availability at home, dummies for household having electricity and a list of dwelling equipments and meal frequency of learner. Figure 1.11 compares the distributions of parental SES by school

Figure 1.11. Stratification of pupils' socio-economic status

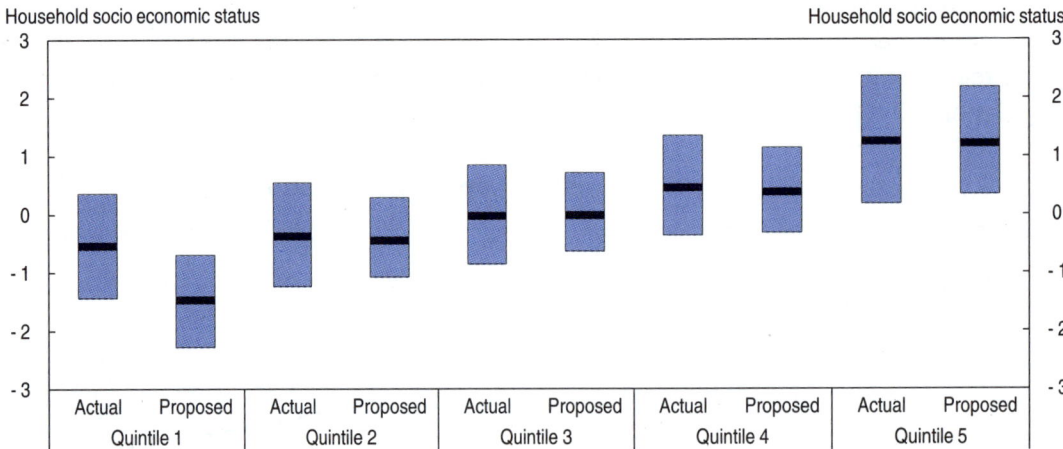

Note: The upper side of each box represents the percentile 75th of the distribution of pupils' parental socio-economic status within each school quintile, while the lower side represents the percentile 25th. The dark line at the center of each box indicates the median.

Source: Department of Basic Education (2009a) and OECD calculations.

StatLink ⟮⟯ *http://dx.doi.org/10.1787/888932783344*

quintile, using alternatively the actual school classification and the one based on median learners' SES. Obviously, these calculations are only illustrative as the survey does not contain all learners at schools. Yet, it is striking that the proposed reclassification of schools would largely allocate most disadvantaged learners to quintile 1, contrary to the current quintile system that does not yield a proper stratification of schools with respect to the social background of learners especially in quintiles 1, 2 and 3 that are almost identical. Moreover, in the proposed reclassification each school quintile would be somewhat more homogenous in terms of pupils social background as shown by the lower distance between the 25th and 75th percentiles in quintiles 2, 3, 4 and 5.

In a few years, the "Information Tracking System" will provide an accurate assessment of schools' socio-economic composition, and will allow for a review of schools classification by quintile based on learners' SES, rather than on geographical location as is currently the case. Under this framework, progressive school funding will be well targeted and should be implemented as soon as possible. In the meantime, the government is right to consider providing equal school funding for all no-fee schools, which almost coincide with schools from the first three quintiles, as pupils' parental SES is not very different across the latter three quintiles. However, the transition towards a truly progressive school funding system based on representative school quintiles should resume rapidly in order to target most the disadvantaged schools in an effective way.

Finally, the existence of school fees in high-SES schools prevents the equalising mechanism described above from working at full strength. The education system remains dualistic with on the one hand a small number of former White schools that can collect tuition fees to supplement teaching and other resources, and on the other hand "no-fee" schools that rely entirely on government funds, do not have enough teachers and generally perform poorly, as shown for instance by the positive relationship between school average performance and school equipment (Figure 1.8). School fees are only 7% of all school resourcing, but in the *Systemic study at grade 9 Survey*, they constitute as much as 45% of top quintile school' budget, versus 2% for quintiles 1 and 2, and 16% for quintile 3.

While school fees have been a way for the government to substitute private for public funding,[3] the dualisation of the education system motivated the introduction of "no-fee schools" in 2007. The share of pupils in "no fee schools" has increased markedly in recent years to reach 69% in 2010, versus 40% in 2007 (Department of Basic Education, 2010a). This is remarkable progress, which has nevertheless only concerned schools relying relatively little on school fees. Any further expansion of the no-fee school policy would be much more costly, especially if additional public funds fully compensated foregone school fees in relatively wealthy schools.

From a long-term perspective, the South African government is encouraged to continue raising the number of no-fee schools in a gradual way, while substituting public for private resources to avoid a collapse of the best-performing schools and a massive flight to private schools. Over the short-term, the phasing-out of school fees could be postponed considering other important issues such as fiscal consolidation.

Increase cost-efficiency through better leadership, accountability and learners support

Improve governance and leadership at the national, local and school levels

The South African education system has been largely decentralised since the South African Schools Act of 1996, which devoted significant powers to School Governing Bodies (SGBs). SGBs include the school principal and elected representatives of parents, teachers and, in secondary schools, students. It is widely recognised, including in a Ministerial Review (cited in OECD, 2008), that SGBs have functioned unevenly due to skill gaps and unequal managing capacities between African and ex-white schools. In particular, provincial authorities still do not have the regulatory power to appoint school principals independently from SGBs recommendations, and cannot dismiss failing school principals, except for serious misconduct.

While greater decentralisation is a desirable objective, it was arguably implemented too early in South Africa given the dysfunctions of SGBs as well as poor local administrative capacity of visiting schools on a regular basis as recalled in the Action Plan to 2014 (Department of Basic Education, 2011b, p. 171). Empirical evidence clearly emphasises that decentralisation and the move towards greater school autonomy do not yield good outcomes when the accountability system is not functioning well, and when local authorities have low capacities (OECD, 2010a). For instance, simple cross-section regressions of average PISA test scores on the degree of school autonomy (which includes funding and/or curriculum autonomy) reveals a strong correlation among countries with developed accountability systems (proxied by the scope of school external inspections, or the use of objective criteria for teacher evaluation) and no correlation among low-accountability countries. Similarly, Hanushek and Woessmann (2013) use panel data evidence on school decentralisation reforms and show that the latter have been conducive to better educational outcomes only among higher-income countries, which have arguably had more experience in designing effective accountability and evaluation systems.

From this point of view, the human and physical resources devoted to the recently-created National Education Evaluation and Development Unit (NEEDU) could be bolstered, as the latter independent team has received a mandate for auditing all levels of the education system in a vertical way (i.e. from national to provincial, district, school and teacher-level effectiveness), thereby assessing the degree of co-ordination among all decentralised members of the country's education system. In years to come, this unit may have a strategic role in designing forthcoming educational reforms based on its ongoing assessment, which should be looked at closely.

Such vertical analysis of the education system is clearly strengthened by the regular implementation of universal and verification Annual National Assessments, first run in 2008, and by the requirement for school leaders to provide school development plans. School principals have also expressed interest in participating in local networks to exchange views on management and pedagogical issues (Taylor et al., 2012). These are crucial innovations that should be nurtured to identify best practices, detect under-performing schools, and improve school leadership (see Box 1.3 on management instruments).

Furthermore South-African based and US evidence shows that strong school principals can have a dramatic positive impact on school performance (Branch et al., 2012; Taylor et al., 2012). Similarly, strategies focusing on school leadership are viewed in a very

> ### Box 1.3. **Management instruments to improve school governance**
>
> **Several management instruments are available at the school level:**
>
> - *School improvement plan*: Each school principal is required to update a school improvement plan annually. In 2008, only 60% of primary schools had a plan, versus 79% overall.
>
> - *School timetable*: 7% of schools did not have a timetable in place according to Integrated Quality Management System (IQMS) monitors.
>
> - *Daily teacher attendance register*: 17% of primary schools did not have updated registers.
>
> - *IQMS instruments* (see teacher evaluation section): Teacher capabilities are evaluated on the basis of self-appraisals, peer-reviews as well as appraisal by a manager of the school. Each school is currently supposed to fill the following IQMS forms: i) appraisals for each teacher; ii) teachers' personal growth plan; iii) school summary score sheet; and iv) internal moderation sheet reflecting on differences between personal and peers appraisals. Only 7% of schools visited have fully implemented the IQMS framework.
>
> - *Annual report*: All schools are required to produce a report reflecting on progress made as envisaged in the school improvement plan. Stronger emphasis on this report is planned in the future.

favourable way to improve school outcomes in disadvantaged schools among OECD countries (OECD, 2012d). Moreover, principal-based strategies are likely to be cost-efficient, as they only require additional resources for a relatively small number of school leaders (about 25 000 in primary and secondary, or 20 times less than the number of teachers). PISA countries with strong school leadership spend available resources more efficiently than other countries, i.e. they maintain a positive correlation between school outcomes (test scores) and expenditure.[4]

School principals' management capacity should be upgraded by increasing participation in the university-based Advanced Certificate of Education (ACE) programme. Moreover, school principals should be appointed after a selective examination process, which would be possible only if the pool of applicants was sufficiently large. To attract highly skilled applicants, wages should be competitive at the national level and additional administrative staff support could be offered.

In turn, school principals should increasingly become accountable for the dynamics of schools' Annual National Assessments, and for the adequacy of their teachers' ratings in the face of audits by external inspectors (see below). Under current institutional settings, the authorities do not have the regulatory power to dismiss the principal of a school where education outcomes are rapidly deteriorating or where serious dysfunctions have been observed. It is therefore crucial that national or competent provincial authorities be available to appoint and/or dismiss school principals in a more flexible way, without School Governing Bodies being able to obstruct the final decision.

Increase teacher monitoring, simplify their evaluation and improve training

Poor teacher quality has been a serious problem, especially in rural areas, where teachers have been reluctant to be redeployed, and as a result, many of the best qualified teachers have left the profession, or have joined fee-paying schools in affluent communities (OECD, 2008). While significant improvements in the administrative qualification of teachers have taken place since 1994, they have had no discernible impact on learning outcomes, which puts in question the value of these qualifications (Department of Basic Education, 2010a). As mentioned above, teachers' cognitive capacities have been put in doubt by the results of formal tests in *SACMEQ 2007 Study* and national surveys (Taylor *et al.*, 2012).

Beyond cognitive skills, low contact time with children or high absenteeism has been a recurrent problem (Spaull, 2012). Many teachers are often late at school, are frequently absent on Fridays, and spend little time on-site. OECD (2008) reports that teachers spend only 46% of their time teaching, while a 70% proportion would be expected on the basis of practice in other countries. Moreover, HIV/AIDS has been a serious concern as about 13% of teachers are HIV-positive (Department of Basic Education, 2010a).

The South African government has decreed many reforms in the area of teachers' accountability, but teacher absenteeism still needs bolder action. Addressing teacher absenteeism could be facilitated by the provision of additional administrative staff dedicated to teacher monitoring. Indeed, recent evidence shows that only 17% of schools maintain up-to-date daily educator attendance registers (Department of Basic Education, 2011b, p. 137). The South African government has the authority to sanction persistent teacher absenteeism by proportional wage cuts. This should be enforced on the basis of updated daily attendance registers. In particular, any fraud in teacher daily attendance registers observed by external inspectors should be detrimental to the administrative staff and school principal, in the form of monetary and/or disciplinary sanctions.

Regarding teachers' wage incentives, it is important to note that the teacher's income distribution is a tightened version of the national income distribution, which means that low-skill teachers are better off than low-skill South-Africans, but that high-skill teachers are worse off than high-skill South-Africans (van der Berg and Burger, 2010). Consequently, the South-African government is rightly considering to align the two above income distributions, first by hiring low-skill primary teachers, who should nevertheless be qualified enough to teach in Foundation Phase, and secondly by introducing wage increases for the best teachers who pass formal examinations of subject knowledge (Department of Basic Education, 2011b). Such increases should be applied in a very selective way to ensure cost-containment of the teacher wage bill, and should target best teachers working in disadvantaged and remote areas, which are the most affected by strong teacher shortage.

Arguably, teacher evaluation could be simplified. The Integrated Quality Management System (IQMS) has been criticised for being too complex and bureaucratic given implementation readiness of a majority of schools (De Clerq, 2008), while the relevance of teacher self-appraisals and personal growth plans in the teacher evaluation process is not striking. In fact, 20% of teachers did not participate in the process in 2009, and only one third of all schools were visited by "moderators" from IQMS. Possibly, evaluation could rely more heavily on school principals' assessments, and periodic external evaluations. While different evaluation models are in place among OECD countries (OECD, 2009a), evaluation based on standardised tests of students do not seem to be adequate given marked social disparities in the country, and the difficulty of properly assessing teachers' "value-added". This *modus operandi* could perhaps be introduced at a later stage.

Assessing the performance of educational actors ultimately serves the purpose of improving teaching quality in the classroom. As explicitly recognised in the Action Plan to 2014 (Department of Basic Education, 2011b), maintaining the right balance between teacher monitoring and support is essential.

Training is the usual way of improving the performance of poor teachers. At the moment, 70% of development activities take place in education departments, while teacher unions, NGOs and universities have also been involved. Regarding training content, the National Education Evaluation and Development Unit is rightly emphasising subject knowledge. Certificated training programmes taking place at university would seem advisable in that regard.

The Action Plan recommends that each teacher follows 80 hours of professional development activities per year, in line with common practice among OECD countries (OECD, 2009b). A new monitoring system run by the South African Council for Educators (SACE) is envisaged to ensure that teachers undertake a sufficient degree of development activities over several years. While ensuring a sufficient quantity of training is a desirable statistical objective, training quality should be the main focus, with the most successful training programmes, such as those taking place at university, being expanded.

It is worth mentioning that the South African government has undertaken a 'Teacher Laptop' initiative, which aims at fostering distance education and training for teachers. As this measure is likely to yield efficiency gains, it is welcome and in line with a recommendation from the OECD 2008 *Education Review* (OECD, 2008).

Finally, teacher peer reviews and teacher local networks are strongly encouraged (OECD, 2009b), as they are deemed to foster the local diffusion of good pedagogical practices. This direction of reform is mentioned in the Action Plan, but practicalities remain to be discussed.

Strengthen core curriculum for disadvantaged learners

Curriculum reform has been unprecedented in scale, substance and style over the last fifteen years (OECD, 2008). A new curriculum known as Curriculum 2005 was launched in 1997. The new curriculum was successfully implemented by historically white schools, but it widened the gap with disadvantaged ones. Following the 2009 curriculum review (Department of Basic Education, 2009b) it has been and will again be simplified. The South African government has rightly sought to adapt the curriculum to existing disparities in resources by giving more emphasis to basic skills in primary schools. The efforts of the government towards better achievement in basic skills could be strengthened by increasing the number of teaching hours in language and mathematics courses among no-fee schools.

Repetition is still high, especially at grades 1, 9, 10 and 11, and should be avoided as it discourages learning. Eliminating grade repetition is actually a major recommendation to foster equity among OECD education systems (OECD, 2012d). South Africa could follow the example of Finland, in which support groups are set up at school to make sure that pupils experiencing difficulties do not fall further behind (OECD, 2012d). Similarly, support teaching should focus on basic skills.

In addition, multi-lingualism is an important contextual difficulty as there is widespread evidence that pupils with an African mother-tongue perform significantly worse in English than Afrikaans speakers. Figure 1.12 reports the distribution of language

Figure 1.12. **Language test scores**

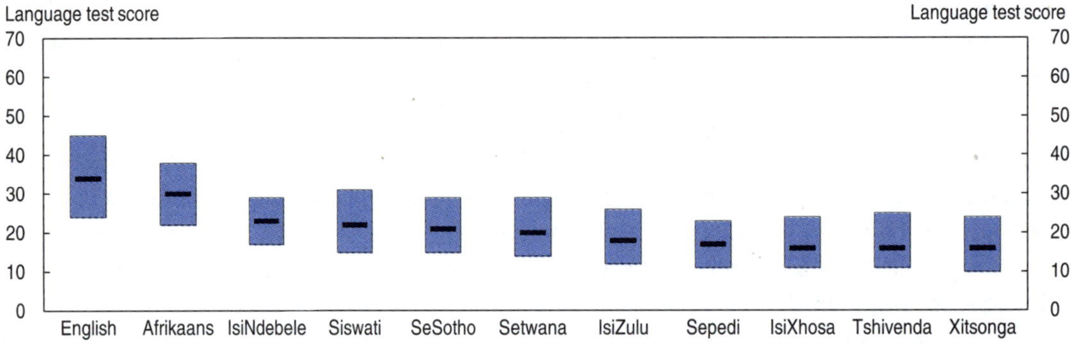

Note: The upper side of each box represents the percentile 75th of the distribution of pupils' language test score by language spoken at home, while the lower side represents the percentile 25th. The dark line at the center of each box indicates the median.
Source: Department of Basic Education (2009) and OECD calculations.

StatLink ⬛ http://dx.doi.org/10.1787/888932783363

scores (English or Afrikaans) from the 2009 systemic study at grade 9 by type of mother-tongue. The upper side of each box represents the 75th percentile, the lower side the 25th percentile, and the black line in the middle of each box indicates the median language test score.

Addressing multi-lingualism would require familiarising learners with English from grade 1 if possible. At the same time, the switch to English as the main language of instruction at grade 4 appears to be highly confusing for unprepared African learners. Ideally, those pupils should be exposed to English in a gradual rather than abrupt way. Strengthening the early teaching of English in most schools would seem a desirable first step, especially in African language schools and at (pre-)primary school level. For instance, only 1% of African language learners study English in grade 1. Expanding the recruitment of English teachers from other (English-speaking) countries such as other African countries or India would be helpful to address pressing and immediate teacher shortages. Regarding the language of instruction, the 'Foundations for Learning' programme, launched in 2008, emphasised the importance of the use of mother-tongue language during the first three years of schooling, a condition that is met by 80% of learners in Foundation phase. The 2009 *Annual Survey of Schools* indicates that, at grade 3, about 70% of learners are taught in an African language, a percentage that drops to 8% at grade 4 (Department of Basic Education, 2011b). In practice, this abrupt switch to English at grade 4 constitutes a very difficult transition for learners, and it could take place in a gradual way or occur later, in line with international practice (OECD, 2012e).

Repairing skill supply and demand mismatch on the labour market

While basic education reforms are necessary to strengthen the education system and increase the general skill level of the population, further reforms of vocational and tertiary education should seek to address high youth unemployment.

Increase the demand for vocational education

High youth unemployment highlights the issue of skill deficiencies among those who fail to pass the matric exam and reach higher education. From that perspective, the vocational education and training system, mostly composed of Further Education and

Training (FET) colleges and Sector Education and Training Authorities (SETAs), appears to be underdeveloped and ill-functioning (OECD, 2008). Public FET colleges accommodate about half a million students while private colleges accommodate about one million students (Lolwana, 2009). Hence, public FET colleges represent less than 10% of pupils enrolled at secondary schools, and display by far the highest pupil-teacher ratios in the education system, although lower teaching time per student in FET colleges may bias the comparison. In practice, technical colleges are characterised by high churning rates as students face important credit constraints and often drop out. The Department of Higher Education and Training (2012, p. 22) reports dropout rates of between 13% and 25%.

South Africa has undertaken important reforms of the VET system, in close connection to the Accelerated and Shared Growth Initiative – "South Africa" (AsgiSA) economic strategy. The key target has been to expand the sector substantially, which is taking place at a reasonably high pace. To this aim, FET colleges have been recapitalised across all provinces, with the objective of upgrading classrooms and staff quality (OECD, 2008). Moreover, the National Skills Strategy III (Department of Higher Education and Training, 2011) introduces a well-articulated development plan. Focusing on a specific part of the vocational system, the expansion of the apprenticeship system, may constitute a useful tool to reduce youth unemployment. Restoring an effective apprenticeship system is an explicit goal of the New Growth Path, which plans for the formation of 50 000 additional artisans by 2014-15.

Successful VET systems in OECD countries, such as the Austrian and German models, often present the dual characteristics of allowing a connection to higher education, which raises the quality of new entrants, and of offering a strong connection to the labour market thanks to up-to-date curriculum in tune with labour market needs (OECD, 2010b, 2012d).

As a first step, the South African government should strengthen the link between FET colleges and university. In Austria, the transfer rate from VET graduates to university was 35% in 2008 (OECD, 2010), but in South Africa, only 15% of college students are able to make the transition to university (World Bank, 2011).

Moreover, some universities are reluctant to recognise credits from these diplomas and obstruct the pathways from post-secondary non-tertiary vocational programmes to higher education (Perold et al., 2012). A tighter connection to higher education would raise the quality of applicants to FET colleges, as the self-selected pool of students in vocational education is often considered to be of lower quality since it encompasses mostly students who were not able to complete the general education cursus.

Furthermore, there is low demand from firms to students graduating from vocational institutions as the curriculum is largely perceived as being outdated (Gewer, 2010). National curricula for vocational programmes have been introduced in 2007, and further reforms are planned in consultation with the business sector. In that regard, the establishment of the South African Institute for Vocational and Continuing Education and Training (SAIVCET), which is to re-build a curriculum with the help of the business sector, is a welcome initiative.

Another way of raising the quality of the curriculum is to develop partnerships between large companies and public or private FET colleges. Indeed, companies invest funds to upgrade the quality of the college in exchange for conveying their views on how to tailor the college curriculum to match their specific needs. There are several anecdotal examples of such partnerships involving foreign companies. It is regrettable that large domestic firms do not engage more in such arrangements.

More generally, strong financial incentives for firms should be put in place to hire trainees from FET colleges. Such incentives could be in the form of tax credit or hiring subsidies for firms hosting the trainees following a vocational cursus in a FET college. At the moment, too little on-the-job training takes place for VET students, as 65% of them are unable to find workplace experience (Department of Higher Education and Training, 2012, p. 26). Training contracted between FET colleges and firms in the context of the vocational cursus concerns an even smaller number of students, about 5%. The integration of workplace training with theoretical training is a goal of the National Skill Development Strategy III, but the latter document does not make explicit the policy levers that would help attain that goal.

Trainees should be hired on a short-term and renewable basis under simplified administrative hiring procedures. While training conditions should comply with labour laws and offer basic working conditions, the current possibility offered to employers to stop training within 21 days after it has started is reassuring as it allows employers to have some minimum influence over trainees' selection. Yet, employers have reported time-consuming informal meetings with administration services of FET colleges, which could be streamlined (Quality Council for Trades and Occupation, 2011).

Finally, emphasis should be put on skills demanded by large and fast-expanding sectors. Figure 1.13 shows that trade, community and social services as well as manufacturing employ large fractions of the workforce and grew at a steady 3% annual rate between 2003 and 2008. Construction and finance sectors are slightly smaller sectors but they expanded rapidly over the same period. While the design of vocational fields should not necessarily stick to the most recent economic trends, which that may change course unexpectedly, the VET system should seek to supply expanding economic sectors with enough technical workers.

Figure 1.13. **Employment distribution and growth by industry**

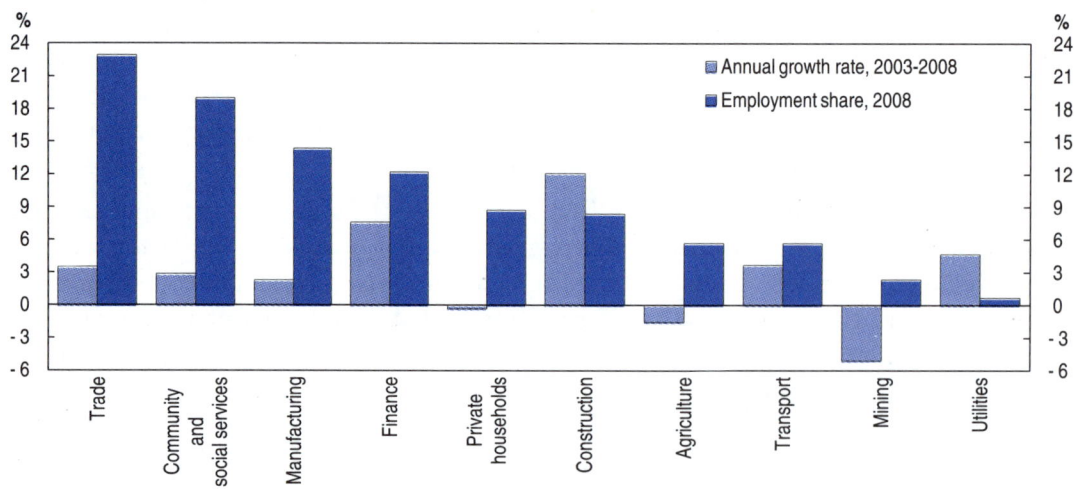

Source: Statistics South Africa (2012), *Labour market dynamics in South Africa.*

StatLink ⬛⬛⬛ *http://dx.doi.org/10.1787/888932783382*

Alleviate credit constraints to raise enrolment at university

Tight credit constraints help explain why enrolment at university has been relatively low (18% of the population aged 18-24) despite very high returns to tertiary education. At the university level, tuition fees are high (about one average monthly wage or ZAR 8 000) and represent 25% of the higher education budget. Recent research conducted by Gurgand *et al.* (2012) has shown that access to loans from private banks significantly raises the probability of enrolling at university. Moreover, Oliveira Martins *et al.* (2009), using panel data evidence, have identified the development of the loans and grants systems as a key determinant of the enrolment rate at university among OECD countries.

The South African government has implemented an income-contingent loan programme (NSFAS) targeted to the poor, which has had a mixed success: in 2009 about 48% of the higher education students that had borrowed from NSFAS had dropped out without completing their studies. As the latter programme is targeting students from lower social background, an additional incentive would be to waive the repayment of the loan in the case of graduating, as rightly envisaged by the South African government. For students with middle social background, greater access to loans from commercial banks would constitute an alternative way of alleviating credit constraints. The government could outsource the management of a large number of income-contingent repayment schemes to private financial companies.

Box 1.4. **Main education recommendations**

Note: Recommendations already contained in OECD (2008) are displayed in italics.

Increase and equalise education resources

- Expand the Accelerated Schools Infrastructure Development Initiative programme to address infrastructure backlogs and *improve the delivery of learning materials* (textbooks, desks, libraries and computers) with priority to the most deprived schools.

- Expand the *Funza Lushaka* bursary programme for teaching studies and allow more immigration of English teachers.

- *Expand the "no-fee school policy"* and *reclassify schools* according to median learners' socio-economic background rather than school location to improve the effectiveness of redistribution.

Strengthen the school leadership strategy

- *Provide more school leadership training and support staff in exchange for stricter accountability.* Allow the education authorities to appoint and dismiss school principals in a more flexible way (depending on progress on school performance in Annual National Assessments and on external reviews), while making school principals responsible for yearly teacher evaluations and monitoring teachers' daily attendance.

- Expand the school principals ACE programme to improve the quality of school management, and develop networks to exchange best-practice experiences among school principals. Maintain strong wage incentives to become a school principal, especially in rural and remote areas.

- Empower the independent federal evaluation unit NEEDU, join the Programme for International Student Assessment (PISA) and the Teaching and Learning International Survey (TALIS) and undertake an OECD *Review of Evaluation and Assessment Frameworks for Improving School Outcomes.*

> ### Box 1.4. **Main education recommendations** (*cont.*)
>
> **Review teacher evaluation and training**
>
> - *Focus on teacher training* on low-performers and subject knowledge.
> - Tie teacher wage increases to selective certificates completion rather than collective or external evaluations.
>
> **Adapt the curriculum to address socio-economic inequalities**
>
> - Expand the focus on basic skills in low-quintile schools and provide support to avoid grade repetition.
> - Introduce English teaching earlier to prepare the learner to the switch to English as the language of instruction. The switch could be gradual or be postponed to a latter grade.
>
> **Remove credit constraints at the tertiary level and improve the VET system**
>
> - Discuss the participation of firms in the elaboration and review of the curriculum.
> - Foster on-the-job training with tax credits and simplify administrative procedures for hiring trainees from FET colleges. Widen the scope for apprenticeship programmes organised by public-private partnerships.
> - Expand the loan system by relying more heavily on private financial companies sub-contracted by the government.

Notes

1. The gross enrolment rate is defined as the number of pupils at school divided by the school-age population. Because of pupils repeating grades, the gross enrolment rate can be larger than 100%. The net enrolment rate is equal to the number of pupils of the expected school-age divided by the school-age population, and hence it is always lower than 100%.

2. Another institutional setting, the Equitable Shares Formula (ESF), focuses on inter-provincial equity. The ESF, which was phased in from 1996 and 2000, calculates the allocation of budgets to provinces based on variables such as the size of the school-age population, the number of learners enrolled in public ordinary schools, the distribution of capital needs, the size of the rural population in each province and the size of the target population for social security grants weighted by a poverty index.

3. Fee-charging schools are subsidised by the government for each disadvantaged child exempted from paying fees, but the subsidy is typically much less than the fees charged to other students, This creates problems as parents who pay fees complain about subsidising children from poorer background and exert pressures on School Governing Bodies, especially in ex-white schools, to regulate access by means of escalating school fees or school language policy.

4. This observation is irrespective of OECD membership and of the normalisation of total education expenditures by GDP per capita.

Bibliography

van der Berg, S. (2006), "How Effective are Poor Schools? Poverty and Educational Outcomes in South Africa", *Stellenbosch University Working Papers*, No. 06/06.

van der Berg, S. and R. Burger (2010), "Teacher Pay in South Africa", *Stellenbosch University Working Papers*, No. 26/2010.

Bhorat, H. and M. Oosthuizen (2008), "Determinants of Grade 12 Pass Rates in the Post-Apartheid South African Schooling System", *Journal of African Economies*, Vol. 18(4), pp. 634-666.

Branch, G., E. Hanushek and S. Rivkin (2012), "Estimating the Effect of Leaders on Public Sector Productivity: The Case of School Principals", *NBER Working Papers*, 17803.

Branson, N. and M. Leibbrandt (2013a), "Educational Attainment and Labour Market Outcomes in South Africa", *OECD Working Paper*, forthcoming.

Branson, N. and M. Leibbrandt (2013b), "Education Quality and Labour Market Outcomes in South Africa", *OECD Working Paper*, forthcoming.

Branson, N., D. Lam, and T. Zuze (2012), "Education: Analysis of the NIDS Wave 1 and 2 Datasets", *National Income Dynamics Study Discussion Papers*, 2012/4, SALDRU.

Case, A. and A. Deaton (1999), "School Inputs and Educational Outcomes in South Africa", *The Quarterly Journal of Economics*, Vol. 114(3), pp. 1047-1084.

Case, A. and M. Yogo (1999), "Does School Quality Matter? Returns to Education and the Characteristics of Schools in South Africa", *NBER Working Papers*, No. 7399.

Colclough, C., G. Kingdon and H. Patrinos (2010), "The Changing Pattern of Wage Returns to Education and its Implications", *Development Policy Review*, Vol. 28(6), pp. 733-747.

Crouch, L. and T. Mabogoane (2001), "No Magic Bullets, Just Tracer Bullets: The Role of Learning Resources, Social Advantage, and Education Management in Improving the Performance of South African Schools", *Social Dynamics*, Vol. 27(1), pp. 60-78.

Crouch, L. and P. Vinjevold (2006), "South Africa: Access before Quality, and What to Do Now?", *Profesorado. Revista de Currículum y Formación del Profesorado*, Vol. 10(1), pp. 5-20.

De Clerq, N. (2008), "Teacher Quality, Appraisal and Development: The Flaws in the IQMS", *Perspectives in Education*, Vol. 26(1), pp. 7-18.

De Lannoy, A. and K. Hall (2012), "Education-Learner to Educator ratio", Children Institute, *www.childrencount.ci.org.za/indicator.php?id=6&indicator=44*.

Department of Basic Education (2009a), *National Assessment of Learner Achievement, Grade 9 Systemic Evaluation*, Pretoria.

Department of Basic Education (2009b), *Report of the Task Team for the Review of the Implementation of the National Curriculum Statement*, Pretoria.

Department of Basic Education (2010a), *Education for All Country Report: South Africa*, Pretoria.

Department of Basic Education (2010b), *School Funding and Management in South Africa: Findings from the School Survey*, Pretoria.

Department of Basic Education (2011a), *Macro Indicators Trends in Schooling: Summary Report*, Pretoria.

Department of Basic Education (2011b), *Action Plan to 2014: Towards the Realisation of Schooling 2025*, Pretoria.

Department of Basic Education (2012), *Questionnaire to the OECD*.

Department of Higher Education and Training (2011), *National Skills Strategy III*, Pretoria.

Department of Higher Education and Training (2012), *Green Paper for Post-School Education and Training*, Pretoria.

Gewer, A. (2010), "Improving Quality and Expanding the Further Education and Training College System to Meet the Need for an Inclusive Growth Path", Development Bank of Southern Africa.

Gurgand M., A. Lorenceau and T. Mélonio (2011), "Student Loans: Liquidity Constraint and Higher Education in South Africa", *PSE Working Papers*, 2011-20.

Hanushek, E., S. Link and L. Woessmann (2013), "Does School Autonomy Make Sense Everywhere? Panel Estimates from PISA", *Journal of Development Economics*, forthcoming.

Hertz, T. (2003), "Upward Bias in the Estimated Returns to Education: Evidence from South Africa", *The American Economic Review*, Vol. 93(4), pp. 1354-1368.

Human Sciences Research Council (2012), *Highlights from TIMSS 2011: The South African Experience*, HSRC press, Pretoria.

Lolwana, P. (2009), "After School, What? Opening Wider and More Flexible Learning Pathways for Youth: Post-compulsory and Post-schooling Provision in South Africa", *Ministerial Committee Final Report*, Pretoria.

Louw, M., S. van der Berg and D. Yu (2006), "Educational Attainment and Intergenerational Social Mobility in South Africa", *Stellenbosch University Working Papers*, No. 09/2006.

National Planning Commission (2012), *National Development Plan 2030*, Pretoria.

OECD (2008), *Reviews of National Policies for Education: South Africa*, OECD Publishing.

OECD (2009a), "Teacher Evaluation: A Conceptual Framework and Examples of Country Practices", from the *OECD Review on Evaluation and Assessment for Improving School Outcomes: Design and Implementation Plan for the Review*, OECD Publishing.

OECD (2009b), *Creating Effective Teaching and Learning Environments: First Results from TALIS*, OECD Publishing.

OECD (2010a), *PISA 2009 Results: What Makes a School Successful? – Resources, Policies and Practices*, Vol. IV, OECD Publishing.

OECD (2010b), *Learning for Jobs: OECD Reviews of Vocational Education and Training – Austria*, OECD Publishing.

OECD (2012a), "Medium and Long-term Scenarios for Global Growth and Imbalances", *OECD Economic Outlook*, Vol. 2012(1), pp. 191-224, OECD Publishing.

OECD (2012b), *OECD Reviews of Evaluation and Assessment in Education: Mexico*, OECD Publishing.

OECD (2012c), *Education at a Glance*, OECD Publishing.

OECD (2012d), *Equity and Quality in Education: Supporting Disadvantaged Students and Schools*, OECD Publishing.

OECD (2012e), *Languages in a Global World: Learning for Better Cultural Understanding*, OECD Publishing.

Oliveira Martins, J., R. Boarini, H. Strauss and C. de la Maisonneuve (2009), "The Policy Determinants of Investment in Higher Education", *Journal: Economic Studies*, Vol. 2009(1), pp. 1-37, OECD Publishing.

Oosthuizen, M. and H. Bhorat (2006), "Educational Outcomes in South Africa: A Production Function Approach", *SISERA Working Paper Series*, No. 2006/5.

Perold, H., N. Cloete and J. Papier (2012), "Shaping the Future of South Africa's Youth", edited by Centre for Higher Education Transformation (CHET), Southern African Labour and Development Research Unit (SALDRU) and the Further Education and Training Institute (FETI), Pretoria.

PIRLS (2006), *International Study Center*, available at *http://timss.bc.edu/*.

Quality Council for Trades and Occupation (2011), "Policy on Delegation of Qualification Design and Assessment to Development Quality Partners and Assessment Quality Partners", online document.

Reddy, V. (2006), *Mathematics and Science Achievement at South African Schools in TIMSS 2003*, HSRC Press, Pretoria.

SACE (2011), "Teacher Migration in South Africa", available at *www.sace.org.za/upload/files/ TeacherMigrationReport_9June2011.pdf*.

SACMEQ III Project (2007), *Southern and Eastern Africa Consortium for Monitoring Educational Quality*.

Simkins, C. and A. Paterson (2005), *Learner Performance in South Africa: Social and Economic Determinants of Success in Language and Mathematics*, HSRC Press, Pretoria.

Spaull, N. (2012), "Poverty and Privilege: Primary School Inequality in South Africa", *Stellenbosch University Working Papers*, No. 13/12.

Statistics South Africa (2007), *Community Survey*, Pretoria.

Statistics South Africa (2011), *General Household Survey*, Pretoria.

Statistics South Africa (2012), *Labour Market Dynamics in South Africa*, Pretoria.

Taylor, N., S.van der Berg and T. Mabogoane (2012), "What Makes Schools Effective? Report of South Africa's National School Effectiveness Study", Pearson Education, Cape Town.

The Economic Development Department (2010), *New Growth Plan*, Pretoria.

TIMSS (2003, 2011), *International Study Center*, available at *http://timss.bc.edu/*.

World Bank (2011), "Background Paper 3: The Role of Higher Education in Closing the Skills Gap in South Africa", Human Development Group, Africa Region.

World Bank (2012), *Online Education Statistics*, available at *http://data.worldbank.org/data-catalog/ed-stats/*.

ANNEX 1.A1

Educational attainment and labour market outcomes

This Annex presents the results from Branson and Leibbrandt (2013a), a paper commissioned by the OECD as background for this *Economic Survey*. Wage and employability premiums associated with different educational levels are calculated for different population groups. Seventeen years of national household survey data spanning 1994 to 2010 are used. The data is compiled from the *October Household Surveys* (OHS's) in the 1990s, the *Labour Force Surveys* (LFS's) between 2000 and 2007 and the *General Household Surveys* (GHS's) for 2008 through 2010. These are currently all the publicly available national household surveys that contain individual level earnings information in addition to individual and household characteristics. The Post Apartheid Labour Market Series (PALMS) version of the 1994-2007 data is used as a starting point and it is supplemented with GHS data in 2008, 2009 and 2010.

The initial model presented is a basic semi log linear wage regression with a quadratic in age (in single years) and education level dummies (the excluded group is those who completed only primary education). Age and age squared are included to account for age and experience since the high rates of grade repetition that characterise the South African schooling system and the high rates of unemployment, especially youth unemployment, limits the appropriateness of the traditional experience specification in the South African context. Formally the model is:

$$\ln(Wage)_i = \alpha_i + \beta_1 Age_i + \beta_1 Age^2{}_i + \gamma_1 IncSec_i + \gamma_2 Matric_i + \gamma_3 Tert_i + \mu_i \ (1) \tag{1}$$

where the dependent variable is the natural logarithm of monthly earnings in South African rand. The model is run for each survey year and an indicator of the month of the survey included for years with more than one survey. This specification is extended to include additional controls for marital status, number of children 0-6 in the household, number of children 7-17 in the household and number of working adults in the household, marital status, number of children and an indicator for urban residence where available (1994-2004). Separate models are run for males and females, and for Africans and total active population.

The results pertaining to education coefficients are reported in Figure 1.A1.1. Estimated coefficients are converted to wage ratios with respect to population with primary only. For instance, the converted coefficient of 2.5 for Africans with a matric in 2010 means that the latter group earns 2.5 times the average wage of Africans who received only primary education.

Figure 1.A1.1. **Wage ratio with respect to population with only primary schooling**

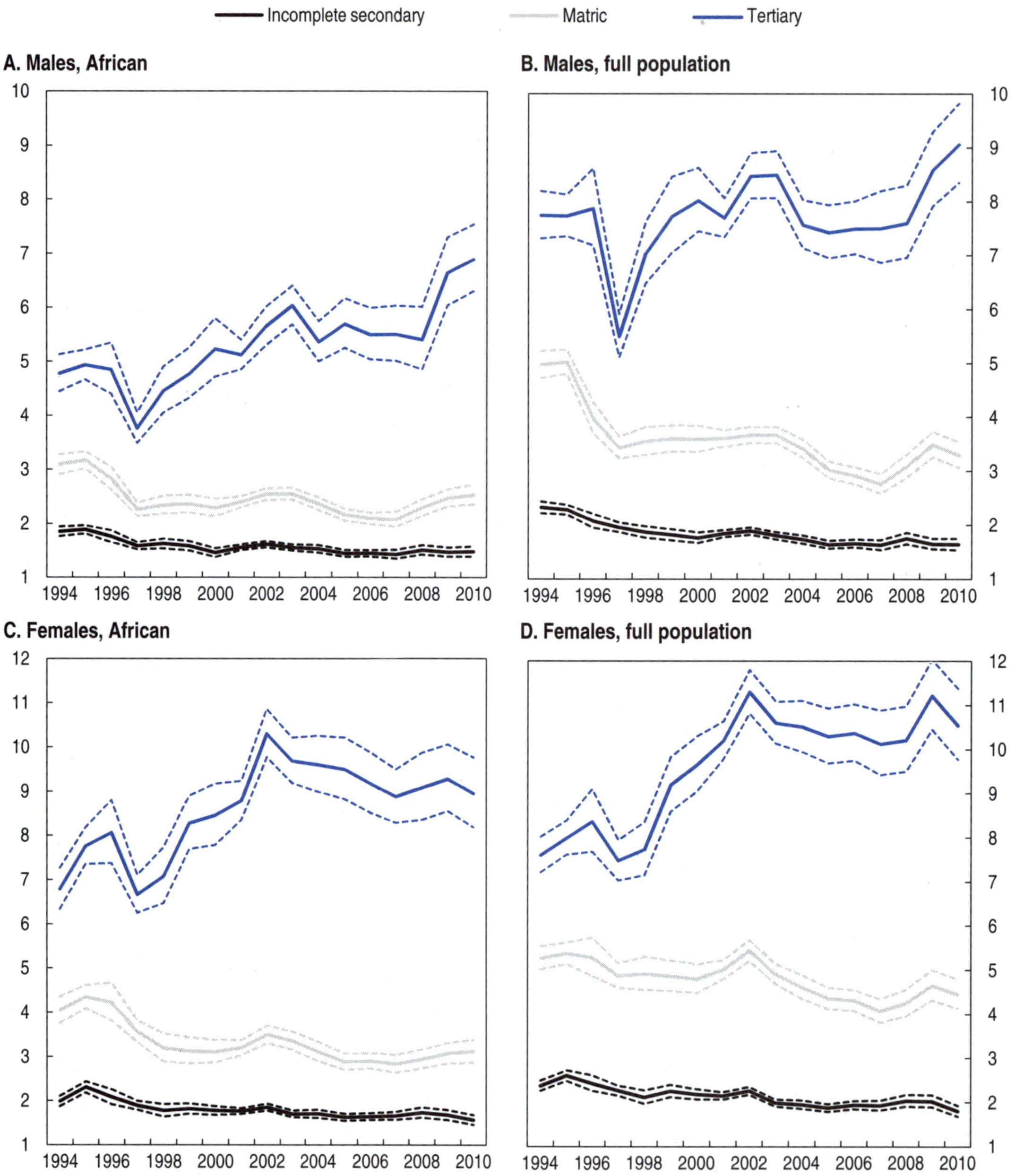

Legend: —— Incomplete secondary   —— Matric   —— Tertiary

A. Males, African

B. Males, full population

C. Females, African

D. Females, full population

Note: This graph presents the converted wage regression coefficients (and confidence bands) on matric (bottom line), incomplete secondary (intermediate line) and tertiary (top line) relative to primary or less obtained from a linear regression of log earnings, controlling for a quadratic in age, marital status, number of children and number of employed adults in the household as well as an indicator of urban residence when available. Converted coefficients = exp(b). All regressions weighted using the cross entropy weights.
Source: Branson and Leibbrandt (2013a).

StatLink ⟐⟐⟐ http://dx.doi.org/10.1787/888932783401

As is evident from Figure 1.A1.1, several results emerge: *i)* Premiums for each education level are higher at the national level than in the African group, which points to the existence of relatively higher returns among Whites, Coloured and Indians; *ii)* The tertiary premium in the national sample is very high while the African tertiary premium, while still high, is lower; *iii)* The premium for tertiary, however, has been increasing for

Africans while it has remained more stable at the national level, except perhaps since 2008; and *iv)* Africans with tertiary education earned almost seven times what Africans with only primary education earned in 2010.

Next the authors investigate the relationship between education level and employment probability. They estimate a linear probability model of the probability of employment given that the individual participates in the labour force:

$$Employed_i = \alpha_i + \beta_1 Age_i + \beta_1 Age^2_i + \gamma_1 IncSec_i + \gamma_2 Matric_i + \gamma_3 Tert_i + \mu_i \quad (2)(2)$$

where the dependent variable indicates whether individuals in the labour force have any form of employment. The authors calculate the increased propensity to be in employment that incomplete secondary, matric and tertiary afford individuals over those with primary or less education graphically. The basic specification includes a quadratic in age, and the controls model supplements this with controls for coloured, Indian, white, married, divorced, widowed, number of children 0-6 in the household, number of children 7-17 in the household, number of working adults in the household and an indicator of urban residence when available

As a result, once household and racial controls are taken into account, only the tertiary employment premium is statistically significant in all years. This means that only those with tertiary have an increased probability of being in employment relative to those with primary education in each year. Males with tertiary are about 10 percentage points more likely to be employed than those with primary. Females with tertiary are about 20 percentage points more likely to be employed than those with primary. The matric coefficient is small in most years and only significantly different from zero in a few years.

ANNEX 1.A2

Education quality and labour market outcomes

This Annex presents the results from Branson and Leibbrandt (2013b), another paper commissioned for this *Economic Survey*. Measures of school quality are included in wage and employment regressions presented in Annex 1.A1. In practice, data from the National Income Dynamic Study (NIDS) are merged with measures of school quality extracted from the Schools Register of Needs and Department of Basic Education matric data on geographic proximity to complete the database.

To reduce the omitted variable bias and endogeneity concerns, the authors focus in the empirical analysis on a particular group, namely prime working-age African adults (aged 32-59 years in 2008) who would have completed their education before the end of apartheid. As mobility of Black Africans was highly restricted during the apartheid regime, allocation of Black African pupils at school may be viewed as exogenous.

Secondly, measurement errors in school quality may attenuate the estimates as the identity of respondents' school during youth is not observed. As a measure of school quality, the pupil/teacher ratio of the respondents' closest high school in place of living during youth is taken as a proxy for the quality of education in the respondents' school. Branson *et al.* (2012) find that over 70% of South African learners in 2008 attend either their closest school or a school within 2 km of their closest school. It is therefore not unreasonable to assume that the closest high school presents a likely option for most respondents, especially given residential restrictions at the time. A similar strategy has been followed by Case and Yogo (1999). As a robustness check, a different proxy for school quality based on the closest high school's pass rate at the matric is considered. Consensus in the US literature is that the measurement error and omitted variable bias are similar in size and cancel each other out (Hertz, 2003).

The empirical specification assumes a direct impact of school quality on earnings or employment:

$$Y_i = \alpha + \beta_1 incomsec_i + \beta_2 matric_i + \beta_3 tertiary_i + \gamma_1 SQ_{is} + X_i'\delta + \varepsilon_i$$

where Y_i is either an indicator of employment or the log of monthly wages, β_1 through β_3 are the coefficients on indicators of whether the respondent has incomplete secondary, matric or tertiary, with primary or no schooling as the reference category. SQ_{is} is a measure of the quality of respondent i's closest high school s, X_i is a matrix of control variables and ε_i is an individual error term. Control variables (X_i) include a quadratic in age, marital status, parental education and urban residence. Note, one would ideally want to control for differences in the mean characteristics of the area where the individual went to school to be assured that the school quality measures are not picking up differences in incomes arising from these differences (*e.g.* average educational level of adults, good health care, parents with jobs, etc.). Controlling for parental education goes some way towards dealing with this. In addition, a full set of dummies for the district council of birth is included to capture unmeasured characteristics of the district council.

As a main result, there is a significant relationship between school quality (be it measured as the pupil-teacher ratio or the matric pass rate) and wages, even after controlling for education level. This relationship is not a function of individual characteristics, parental education or other unobserved characteristics of the district council in which the respondent was born. The size of the coefficient actually increases with the addition of controls and the district council of birth fixed effects. A one pupil reduction in the pupil/teacher ratio results in a 1% increase in earnings.

There is less evidence of a relationship between school quality and employment than was seen between school quality and wages. As was found for the wage regressions, the size and significance of the coefficients on the educational categories are similar to national data analysis: only tertiary is found to have a significant effect on employment. The inclusion of the quality measure does not impact the education coefficients substantially.

School quality appears to play less of a direct role in determining employment than it does in determining wages. The matric pass rate is significant in all specifications, while the pupil-teacher ratio is significant only when it interacts with attained educational level variables. In this case, reducing the number of learners under the responsibility of one teacher by 10 learners improves the employment probability by 0.03.

ANNEX 1.A3

The determinants of pupils tests scores at grade 9

This Annex presents joint work, soon forthcoming as an OECD working paper, with the South African Human Sciences Research Council (HSRC) on the determinants of pupils' performance in mathematics, language (English or Afrikaans) and science national test scores at grade 9 (Department of Basic Education, 2009a). The data set is built on seven questionnaires: three are administered to learners before they answer the language, mathematics and natural science tests respectively, three are answered by the teachers of the tested subjects and the last one is filled in by the school principal. There are three dependant variables, corresponding to the test scores in language, mathematics and science. To exploit the raw answers from the seven questionnaires, a preliminary stage of data consolidation was conducted to extract relevant information in the most efficient way. New indicators were created by regrouping questions dealing with a similar subject and by applying principal component analysis in order to construct a more manageable set of variables.

A large number of potential explanatory variables (about 100) is considered. A Bayesian algorithm allows to select the set of variables that are the most robustly associated with test scores among a high number of potential candidate variables. Remaining endogeneity concerns would ban strictly causal interpretation of the above results, but the high number of control variables and the severity of the Bayesian robustness analysis conducted on the data reduce the risk of endogeneity bias.

A Bayesian Model Averaging (BMA) framework is able to select the set of most robust explanatory variables. The goal of the algorithm is to find a subset of variables X_γ that significantly affects the scores, i.e. to find the "best" relation with the structure:

$$y = \alpha_\gamma + \beta_\gamma X_\gamma + \varepsilon \quad \varepsilon \sim N(0, \sigma^2 I)$$

with y being the test score, α_γ a constant, β_γ the coefficients and ε a normal error term of variance σ^2. One possible approach is to start with the full set of possible variables (here very large), and to suppress non-significant terms, but this process is neither very robust nor efficient. BMA uses Bayesian theory to tackle this issue. The broad idea is to start with a prior on which model is the most likely and estimate a posterior probability applying Bayesian rule. If M_γ denotes the model with regressors X_γ, this posterior model probability (PMP) is, by Bayesian rule:

$$PMP_\gamma = p(M_\gamma | y, X) = \frac{p(y | M_\gamma, X) p(M_\gamma)}{p(y | X)}$$

As $p(y|X)$ is constant over models, the PMP is the proportional to the model prior $p(M_\gamma)$ times the marginal likelihood of the data given the model $p(y|M_\gamma, X)$. The idea of BMA is then to use these PMPs as weights to infer average posterior distribution of the coefficients:

$$p(\beta|y, X) = \sum_\gamma PMP_\gamma . p(\beta|y, X, M_\gamma)$$

Several different priors have been tested and deliver comparable results. Many variables have close to zero coefficients when they have negligible probability of inclusion. The magnitude of coefficients is assessed by calculating the change in test scores (as a share of the standard deviation of test scores) when increasing each variable by one standard deviation.

Regarding policy variables, school equipment is an important factor of learners' outcome. There are large effects associated with a library or ICT laboratories. Having a pupil-teacher ratio above 25 has a significant, negative and large impact in some regressions, but it is not selected as a robust variable by the algorithm. Other large effects were found for contextual variables such as provincial dummies, native language, parental literacy, good nutrition, and distance to school. It is worth noting that the above mentioned factors seems to explain most of the gap observed between population group, as the population effect (capturing other unobserved factors correlated with race) is rather weak, at least in language. There is no statistical link between qualification and training of personnel and learner outcomes, an unexpected finding that may be explained by measurement errors in the latter variables.

Chapter 2

Economic growth in South Africa: Getting to the right shade of green

Despite having become increasingly active in the area of green growth policies, and despite having put in place a generally sound environmental policy framework, South Africa needs to improve implementation to meet key environmental challenges. Effective green growth policies should be combined with other structural and macroeconomic policies to reconcile rapid economic growth with environmental sustainability. A key element of such a policy mix is improving price-setting in the key areas of greenhouse gas emissions and water. The South African economy is very carbon-intensive, in part because of implicit subsidies to coal and electricity, while there is as yet no economy-wide carbon price to internalise environmental externalities. More generally, not all instruments to achieve the government's commitments on emissions abatement are in place, and progress on implementation of the instruments that have been identified has been slow. The monitoring of progress and the verification of coherence between different initiatives should be improved. South Africa is already a water-scarce country, and water stress will worsen with population growth and climate change. The existing policy framework is broadly consistent with best international practice, but implementation has lagged. In general, charges for water need to rise to be increase cost recovery and price scarcity, while the allocation of licenses should be speeded up, municipal management strengthened and illegal water use curtailed.

South Africa has become increasingly active as regards policies to deliver green growth

Why care about the greenness of growth?

Given the scale of unemployment and the negative consequences that flow from it, raising employment is undoubtedly the highest immediate priority for economic policy in South Africa. Increasing employment by enough to bring unemployment down decisively will require rapid economic growth over a number of years. In designing policies to achieve that key objective, however, policy-makers need to gauge the risk that the pattern of current growth undermines social welfare in the future. One aspect of this risk relates to a loss of social cohesiveness – too great a widening in the distribution of income and wealth may ultimately disrupt the stability of the economy and curtail growth. Another, the subject of this chapter, is that environmental degradation becomes a constraint on the growth of income and well-being. Coping with this environmental risk while achieving strong growth rates is central to green growth.

As noted in the National Development Plan, for more than a century South Africa exploited its natural resources with little regard for the environmental consequences. The legacy of that approach was an energy-intensive economy highly dependent on cheap coal and polluted air and water from mining and industry. South Africa faces many environmental challenges, including waste management, local air and water pollution, pressures on biodiversity and marine resource management. The forthcoming OECD *Environmental Performance Review of South Africa* will address the full panoply of environmental issues. Two policy questions – climate change and the scarcity of clean water – are of particular importance for the wellbeing of South Africa's population and future economic development, however, and are thus picked out as the focus of this chapter.

These two challenges are interrelated. Notably, climate change is expected to increase the degree of water stress via a higher frequency of extreme weather events including droughts and floods. Action to mitigate climate change could also help more directly to ease water stress: a lower-carbon mix of electricity generation technologies would reduce water use at the margin, as coal-burning plants both emit more carbon dioxide per unit of energy produced than other plants and use more water – coal-fired power stations account for about 7% of non-agricultural water consumption. In addition, a substantially higher relative price of electricity, in part driven by climate change considerations, will reduce overuse of water by weakening the incentive for farmers to use electricity to pump groundwater. Likewise, success in managing water demand could reduce the future need for energy-intensive water supply options like desalination of sea water.[1] In both cases, climate change and water management, the authorities are working towards the expanded use of pricing of externalities to encourage a more economically efficient use of resources, but face important challenges of implementation.

The South African authorities are fully aware of these environmental challenges, and have increasingly embraced green growth policies. To date, given that employment creation is a critical priority, there has been an understandable emphasis on the scope for job creation in the green economy. The New Growth Path (NGP), for example, targets the creation of 300 000 green jobs by 2020, and the Industrial Policy Action Plan (IPAP) identifies the green economy as one of three priority areas for scaling up.

Although this sort of line may be effective as a strategy to sell green growth to sceptical stakeholders, it is not without risks. To begin with, it is likely to exaggerate the scope for "win-win" opportunities which boost growth, even in the short run, while curbing environmental harm. It may thus court disappointment and ultimately even discredit green-oriented policies in the eyes of the public if the growth and employment gains are not forthcoming on the promised scale. Such an approach may also tend to lead to a muddling of objectives, with green growth initiatives being judged mainly on their perceived employment potential rather than their contribution (and the cost effectiveness of that contribution) to sustainability. Meanwhile, it may distract attention from the many other policy measures needed to deliver satisfactory growth rates in South Africa: notably, promoting competition, improving the functioning of labour markets, maintaining the right macroeconomic policy mix and creating favourable framework conditions for investment and innovation. In addition, there is a danger of counting only direct job gains from a given measure (e.g. subsidised production of renewable energy) and not any associated job losses elsewhere or indirect effects (Bowen, 2012).

Rather than focussing on the (in any case hard-to-define) "green economy" and "green jobs", it may be preferable to stress the more direct welfare case for engaging in policy interventions to promote greener growth. This is above all that since various environmental harms are not reflected in market prices, in the absence of policy interventions such harms will be oversupplied and the well-being of the population will be lower. This is in line with the OECD's Green Growth Strategy (OECD, 2011a), which notes that at the core of green growth are constraints or distortions in the economy which inhibit returns to "green" investment and innovation, i.e. activities which can foster economic growth and development while ensuring that natural assets continue to provide the resources and ecosystem services on which our well-being relies.

The key policy issues are to develop a transition toward a greener economy and a set of policies that will deliver this path. In this context, two policy questions to be answered are how much greener growth should be (i.e. at what point would the expected marginal benefits of increasing the greenness of growth be equal to the expected marginal costs) and how to minimise the cost of achieving the targeted shade of green. Given the high degree of uncertainty in this area, governments should be concerned with not only maximising the expected value of social welfare, but also avoiding very bad outcomes. The Stern Review (Stern et al., 2006) drew attention to the risk of catastrophic climate change and argued that the cost of greatly reducing that risk was low. This sort of argument may be of particular importance for a middle-income country like South Africa, which has environmental and social vulnerabilities that make it less resilient than most advanced countries.

It will be necessary to improve the measurement of environmental costs and benefits

Especially given the extent of uncertainty about the long-term costs of a "Business as Usual" approach and the size and timing of the benefits of greening growth, it is also important to fill the knowledge gaps to the extent possible. One avenue to this end is to improve alternative measures of well-being. While it is clear that GDP is an incomplete and imperfect gauge of social welfare, in the absence of a better alternative it continues to be the single most used indicator of living standards. Moving beyond GDP is an area where an increasing amount of theoretical and empirical work has been done (*e.g.* Stiglitz *et al.*, 2010). The OECD has been in the forefront of such efforts (OECD, 2011b), and has created the Better Life Index to illustrate how we might get a better picture of social welfare by combining different indicators, with user-determined weights. Better Life Index data are not yet available for South Africa – only OECD member countries and two non-members, Russia and Brazil, are covered to date.

A worthwhile long-term objective would be to develop and publish national accounts measures that factor in natural resource depletion and the costs of environmental degradation, although this is likely to take time, as such efforts are in their infancy even in more developed countries. South Africa has already made some preliminary efforts to measure resource use, however, via a number of Environmental Economic Accounts. Statistics South Africa has issued discussion documents for energy, minerals and water, providing energy accounts for the period 2002-09, mineral accounts for 1980-2009, and water accounts for the year 2000.[2] These efforts have not yet made it possible to integrate the environmental accounts with the national accounts, so as, for example, to adjust GDP growth for all resource use. In addition, they rely on the irregular provision of data from other government ministries, are not always in line with national accounts classifications (*e.g.* as regards the Standard Industrial Classification of economic activities) and in some cases are limited to physical volumes. Nonetheless, these discussion documents have added to the understanding of natural resource use and sustainability, and progress towards the issuance of regular and complete Environmental Economic Accounts should continue.

South Africa has also made some progress on the creation of sustainability indicators, including at the provincial level. Both the national government and the provinces are obliged to provide periodic State of the Environment reports – the last national State of the Environment report was in 2006. It could be useful for the authorities, and for international comparisons, if South Africa were to monitor the limited set of Headline Indicators and the broader range of measures proposed in the OECD's Green Growth Indicators (OECD, 2011c, 2012b).

If official adjustments to the national accounts to take account of resource depletion and environmental harm are still some way off, estimates from elsewhere are already available. The World Bank's Adjusted Net Saving indicator seeks to show the extent to which a country adds to its wealth, *i.e.* its capacity to generate income, in a given period by adjusting nominal saving by additions to human capital and degradation of the stock of natural resources. A negative number for Adjusted Net Saving indicates a decline in the economy's capacity to generate income, implying an unsustainable path. Compared to other middle-income countries, as well as other resource-rich countries like Australia and Canada, South Africa's adjusted net saving in 2008 was strikingly low (Figure 2.1A). It has also been on a downtrend since the early 1990s (Figure 2.1B), owing mainly to rising energy (coal) and mineral depletion. While the adjusted net saving measure is neither comprehensive nor universally accepted (Neumayer, 2000), South Africa's low relative position and negative trend on this metric are a *prima facie* cause for concern.

Figure 2.1. **Adjusted net saving**

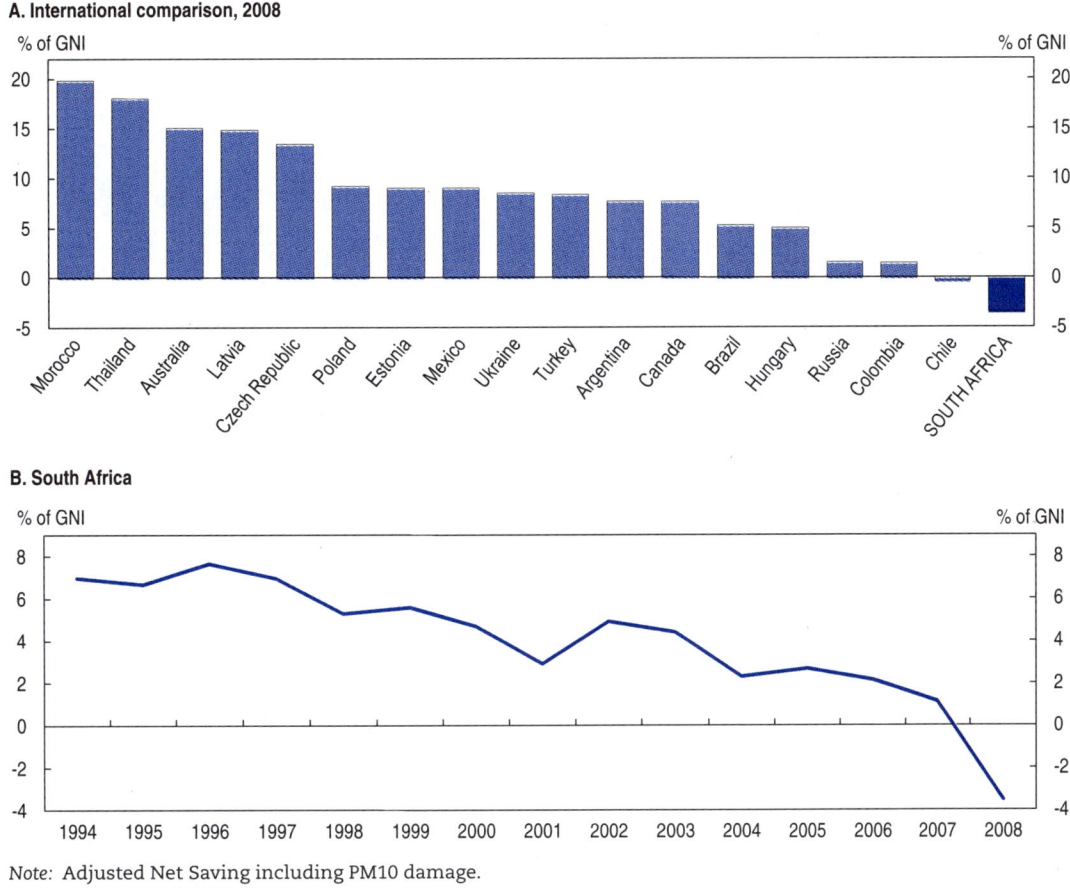

Note: Adjusted Net Saving including PM10 damage.
Source: World Bank, WDI Database.

StatLink ⟍ http://dx.doi.org/10.1787/888932783420

The high environmental cost of growth in the past in South Africa and the tentative evidence that national wealth, the basis for future income, is currently being run down highlight the need to increase the degree of decoupling of growth from natural resource use. Only in that way can the sorts of growth rates targeted in the National Development Plan and the New Growth Path be consistent with sustained increases in well-being of the population.

Getting green policies right involves balancing several instruments at different levels

Governments can advance green growth in various ways, including "green taxes", which South Africa already uses fairly extensively (Figure 2.2), tradable permits, regulation, and support for eco-innovation. Instruments that rely on price signals often have a cost-effectiveness advantage, as this tends to have more decentralised information requirements and equalises the marginal cost of abating a given harm. Sometimes, however, it may be infeasible or too costly to create prices that are not established by the market, making it necessary to resort to other instruments such as regulatory standards.

Apart from technical difficulties, policy-makers face the political economy challenge of taking policy actions that are strong enough to change behaviour and trigger entrepreneurial responses, but not so strong as to create insuperable political resistance. A number of OECD economies, including Australia, the European Union and Norway, have

Figure 2.2. **Environmentally related tax revenues, per cent of GDP**

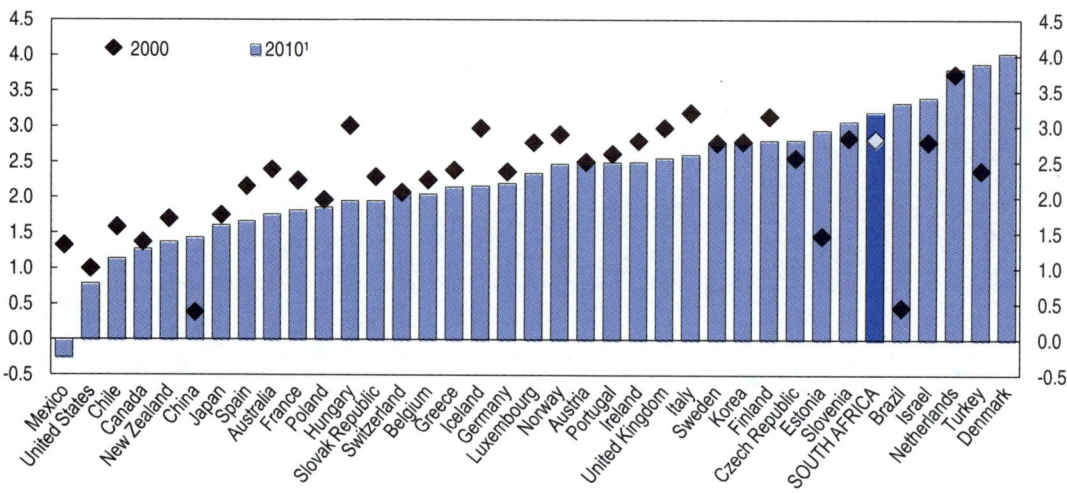

Explanatory note: Tax revenues are shown net of subsidies, which is why Mexico is shown as having negative environmental related tax revenues. In the case of South Africa no subsidies are deducted from gross tax revenues, as the below-market pricing of coal and electricity are not reflected in budgetary allocations.
1. 2009 for Canada, Greece and the Slovak Republic.
Note: Environmentally related taxes include taxes on energy products (for transport and stationary purposes including electricity, petrol, diesel and fossil fuels), motor vehicles and transport (one-off import or sales taxes, recurrent taxes on registration or road use, other transport taxes), waste management.
Source: OECD Green Growth Indicators Database.

StatLink ᵜᶦᶳᴾ *http://dx.doi.org/10.1787/888932783439*

been relatively successful in meeting that challenge. And within the EU countries like Germany have achieved a high degree of buy-in to environmental goals. In South Africa, the political economy challenge has two important dimensions: providing adequate protection to the large number of poor people and overcoming the resistance of large and powerful enterprises.

In addition, many environmental policy instruments may be applied at different levels of government, and co-ordinating policy across those levels raises a number of difficulties (Box 2.1).

Box 2.1. Multi-level environmental governance in South Africa

South Africa's Constitution designates the environment as an area of concurrent national and provincial responsibility, *i.e.* both the national and provincial governments have the power to make and implement environmental legislation. In case of conflict, national environmental legislation prevails over provincial norms and standards. Along with more recent provincial environmental laws (*e.g.* Limpopo Environmental Management Act, 7/2003), the provincial authorities administer historical conservation and land-use planning ordinances (often fragmented substantively as well as territorially) that were applied to apartheid-era homelands, as well as environmental functions delegated to them by the national executive bodies. The management of surface water, groundwater and marine resources as well as national parks are the exclusive competence of the national government.

Box 2.1. **Multi-level environmental governance in South Africa** (*cont.*)

While the stringency of environmental requirements does not vary dramatically across the provinces, significant discrepancies exist between the provinces with respect to the implementation of the national laws. The operational guidelines and actual practices often show the different levels of stringency, *e.g.* with respect to Environmental Impact Assessment procedures and environmental authorisations. At the same time, provinces sometimes undertake initiatives in policy areas where they do not have legal competencies without waiting for national-level programmes (*e.g.* in water resources management).

South Africa has undertaken an ambitious decentralisation programme in order to empower local authorities. The functional expansion of local government authority (including the provision of such environmental services as water supply, sanitation and waste management) has been one of the most significant institutional changes in South Africa since the end of apartheid. Local governments now have the competence for such environmental issues as air pollution, noise pollution, water supply and sanitation, storm-water management, and non-toxic solid waste management. Local authorities also play an important role in regulating land use and development through monitoring and enforcing compliance with relevant zoning regulations.

While the legislation does not provide for the differentiation of environmental responsibilities among the 278 municipalities, the functions they actually exercise depend on their size and capacity. The eight large metropolitan municipalities (Category A) are usually well equipped to execute their environmental mandate and generally have fairly stringent by-laws on air pollution and waste management. The 45 district municipalities (Category B) often assume the functions of smaller local (rural) municipalities (Category C) located in their districts. The exercise of local government powers is subject to national and provincial oversight in order to address capacity gaps and prevent potential mismanagement. For example, the provinces may assume certain regulatory responsibilities if the municipalities lack capacity to execute them: three provinces currently deal with air quality issues which are normally part of the municipalities' remit.

Following the constitutional principle of "co-operative governance" and the provisions of the 2005 Intergovernmental Relations Act, South Africa has established mechanisms and procedures to promote the co-operation between the national, provincial and local governments and to facilitate the settlement of intergovernmental disputes. They include the MINMECs – standing intergovernmental bodies that consist of sectoral Ministers and Members of provincial Executive Councils responsible for functional areas similar to those of Ministers, MINTEC – Directors-General and the heads of the provincial departments and issue-specific working groups. Those seem to be particularly effective in the collaboration between different levels of government on environmental compliance and enforcement. However, an effective implementation of environmental policies is hampered by an important lack of institutional capacity at the provincial and local levels, among others, in terms of environmental management. Most provinces have declining environmental budgets, environmental staff are over-committed and are rarely engaged in horizontal or vertical interagency co-operation. In addition significant discrepancies exist between the provinces, and even greater ones across municipalities, with respect to the implementation of the national legal environmental requirements. The funding gap between the available resources and the needs to meet programme objectives is more acute in smaller, rural, less economically developed jurisdictions, contributing to inequities of policy implementation.

Meeting the challenge of climate change

The economy is carbon-intensive, in part because of implicit subsidies to coal and electricity

South Africa is towards the upper end of the international range in terms of greenhouse gas (GHG) emissions per capita, and among the most emission-intensive middle-income countries (Figure 2.3). Of the 134 countries for which IEA data are available, South Africa ranked 47th in 2008 in per capita greenhouse gas emissions, with 10.3 tonnes of CO_2 equivalent, 43% above the global mean. Even compared to upper-income countries, South Africa is close to the average: 11 of 34 OECD countries have lower greenhouse gas emissions per capita.

Unlike most developing countries, South Africa has a long history of relatively high GHG emissions – per capita emissions were already in the middle of the range for OECD countries in the early 1970s. Also, the growth of emissions picked up to 2.5% a year in the 2000s compared to 1.3% in the 1990s. This reflected an acceleration in the rate of increase of GDP, but South Africa experienced less decoupling than most other countries in the 2000s (Figure 2.4).

Figure 2.3. **Greenhouse gas emissions per capita**

A. South Africa's emissions are high for a middle income country

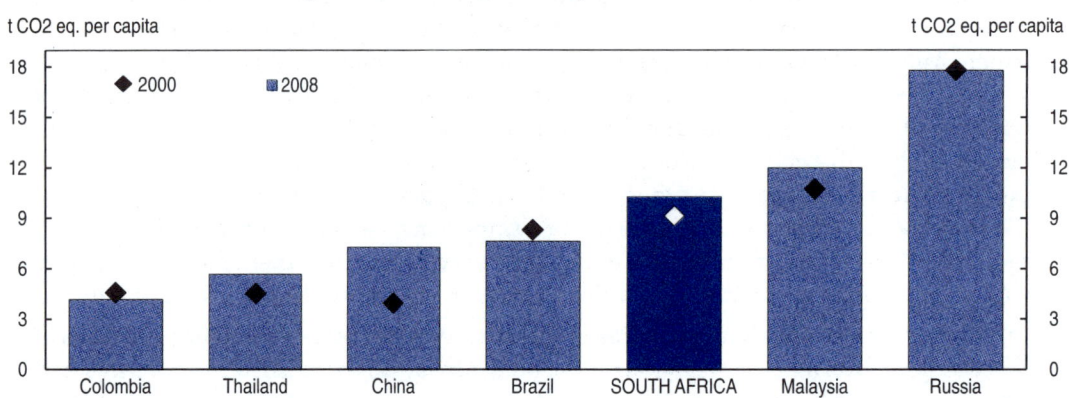

B. Many OECD countries have lower emissions per capita

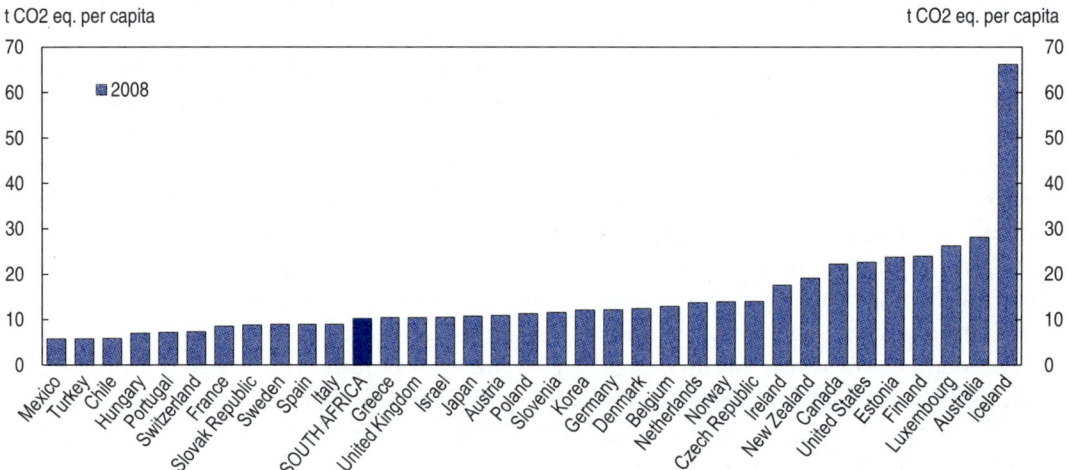

Source: IEA (2011) and World Bank, *WDI Database on line.*

StatLink ⟶ http://dx.doi.org/10.1787/888932783458

Figure 2.4. **Degree of decoupling of emissions and real GDP**

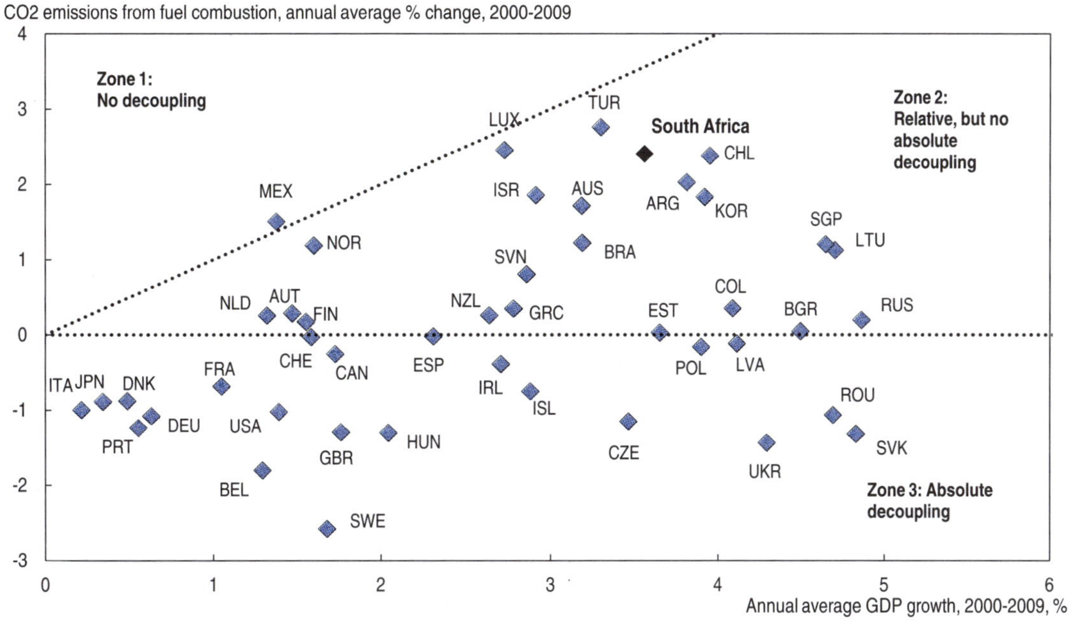

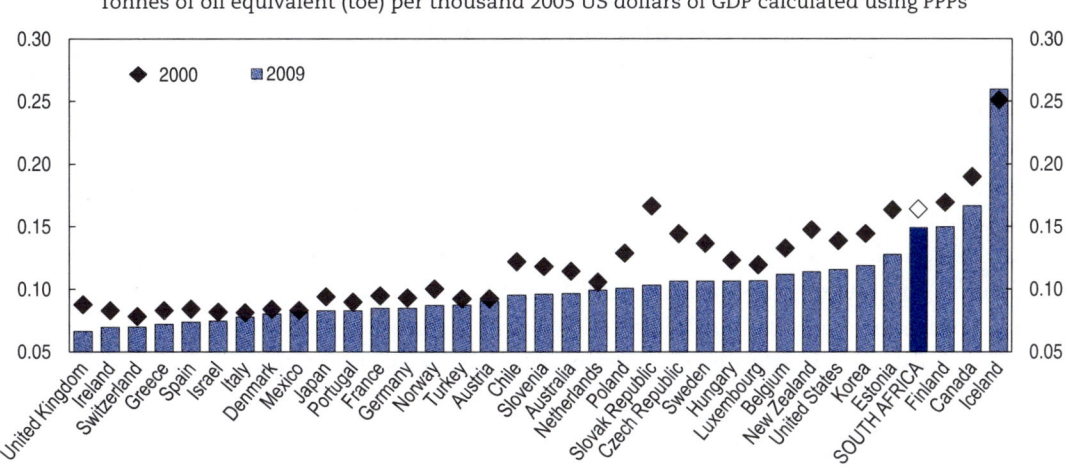

CO2 emissions from fuel combustion, annual average % change, 2000-2009

Source: OECD National Accounts Database; World Bank, WDI online Database; and IEA(2011), CO_2 Emissions from fuel combustion.

StatLink ⫘ http://dx.doi.org/10.1787/888932783477

South Africa's relatively high emissions partly reflect the energy intensiveness of the economy. Primary energy use per unit of GDP is among the highest in the world (Figure 2.5), and has fallen less rapidly than both advanced and developing countries: from 2000 to 2009, energy intensity of GDP fell by 9% in South Africa compared to 14% for OECD countries on average and 24% for an average of Brazil, China, India, Indonesia and Russia (Figure 2.6).

Figure 2.5. **Total energy consumption per unit of GDP**

Tonnes of oil equivalent (toe) per thousand 2005 US dollars of GDP calculated using PPPs

Source: IEA, World Energy Balances Database and OECD, National accounts Database.

StatLink ⫘ http://dx.doi.org/10.1787/888932783496

Figure 2.6. **Total energy consumption per unit of GDP, 2000-09**

Tonnes of oil equivalent (toe) per thousand 2005 US dollars of GDP calculated using PPPs

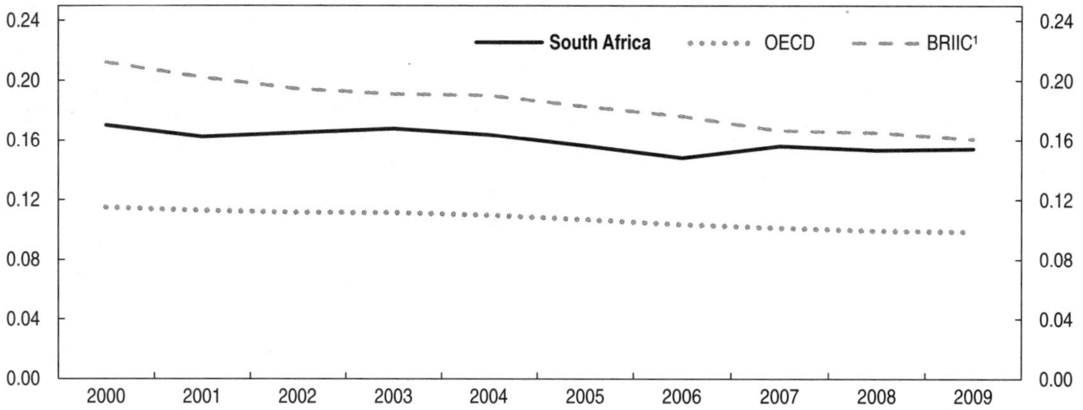

1. Brazil, Russian Federation, India, Indonesia and China.
Source: IEA, *World Energy Balances Database*; OECD, *National accounts Database*; and World Bank, *WDI Database*.
StatLink ᴹˢ⚏ http://dx.doi.org/10.1787/888932783515

The most important reason for the high emissions intensity of the South African economy, however, is the extremely high share of coal in electricity generation. About 92% of electricity generation is fuelled by coal, with nuclear power accounting for approximately 6% and hydro power 2%. As a result, average CO_2 emissions for power generation are around 1 kg/kWh, some 60% higher than the world average. Electricity generation produces over half of total greenhouse gas emissions in South Africa.

The high energy intensity of the economy and the dominance of coal in the power generation mix largely reflect South Africa's resource endowments: the local abundance of coal and other mineral resources, which result in a relatively large role for energy-intensive mining and processing. It is also, however, a function of domestic prices of electricity having been excessively low for a long period. After a build-up of excess generation capacity in the 1980s, investment was dormant until the last few years, and long-term contracts with very low electricity prices were used to attract foreign investment in smelting operations (using imported ore) in the 1980s and 1990s. Current costs were relatively low, depreciation became a minor factor as plants aged, and domestic prices were not reflective of the capital costs necessary to expand capacity in the future.

From already low levels the price of electricity fell in real terms by almost half between the early 1980s and the low point in 2003, much more than the OECD average and in contrast to other middle-income countries like Mexico and Turkey (Figure 2.7). For many years South Africa therefore enjoyed some of the lowest electricity prices in the world. Indeed, although prices started rising sharply in 2008 (Figure 2.8), after a series of outages sparked an emergency response, as of 2011 South Africa still had extremely low electricity tariffs compared to other middle-income countries as well as advanced economies (Figure 2.9). Eskom, the state-owned power utility that produces almost all of South Africa's electricity, estimates that current electricity prices are still only about two thirds of the level needed to cover total costs, including capital costs, even though average prices have more than doubled in real terms since 2007.

A key reason why current costs have long been very low in South Africa is that Eskom has been able to buy domestic coal at average prices well below its alternative use. Much of Eskom's coal is supplied by captive collieries or under medium-term contracts which have

Figure 2.7. **Evolution of electricity prices for industry, selected countries**

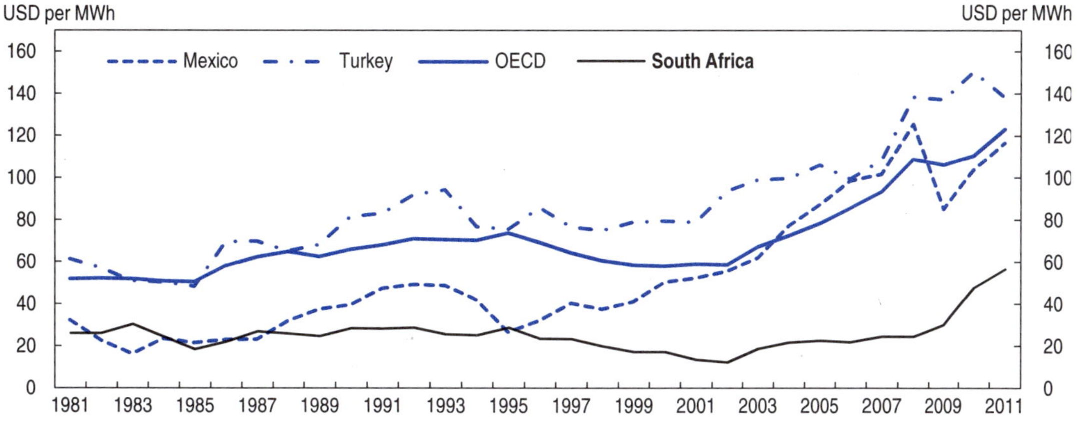

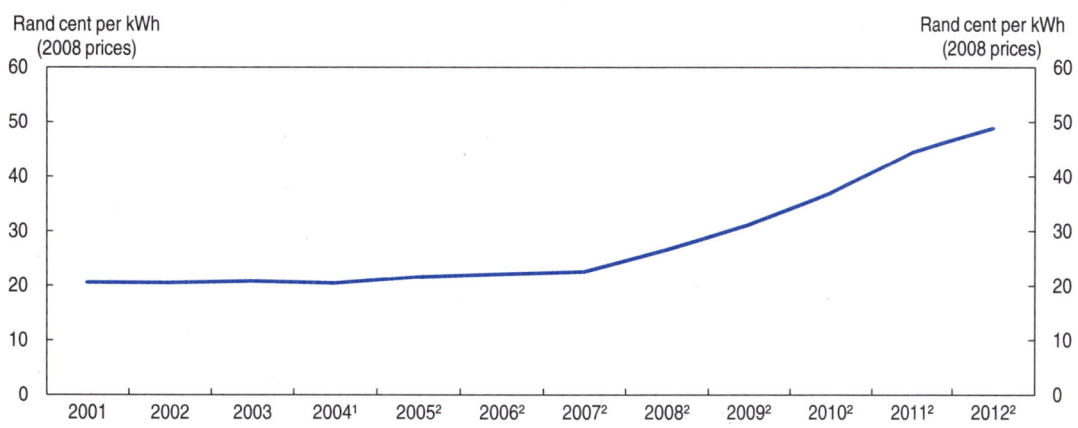

Source: IEA, *Energy prices & Taxes Database* and Eskom.

StatLink http://dx.doi.org/10.1787/888932783534

Figure 2.8. **Real average electricity price**

1. Period covered = 1 Jan 2004 to 31 March 2005.
2. Financial year = 1 April to 31 March.
Note: The real price is calculated by deflating the nominal price by the consumer price index.
Source: OECD estimates based on *Eskom 2012, 2010, 2006 and 2003 Annual Reports*.

StatLink http://dx.doi.org/10.1787/888932783553

on average been much lower than the export price of coal. One factor facilitating this situation is the limited capacity in rail transport and ports, which are both dominated by another state-owned enterprise, Transnet. This constraint has prevented coal being diverted to exports and forcing Eskom's buying prices to rise to international levels (adjusted for transport costs). Eskom's average coal purchase price is around ZAR 200 per tonne (USD 23), which is only about one fifth of the export price, depending on quality. Although quality differences may make the comparison somewhat misleading, an upper bound on the implied subsidy to Eskom is some two thirds of its total revenue, which is equivalent to more than 2½ per cent of GDP. Regardless of the exact magnitude of the implicit subsidy, it is clear that not only do current electricity prices still fail to cover operational and capital costs, but operational costs are artificially depressed to a considerable degree by Eskom's access to below-market-price coal.

The underpricing of coal and electricity has amounted to a large negative carbon tax, which is to say a subsidy to CO_2 emissions. Also, apart from giving rise to a relatively large

Figure 2.9. **Electricity price, international comparison**
2011 or latest year available, USD per MWh

A. Electricity for industry

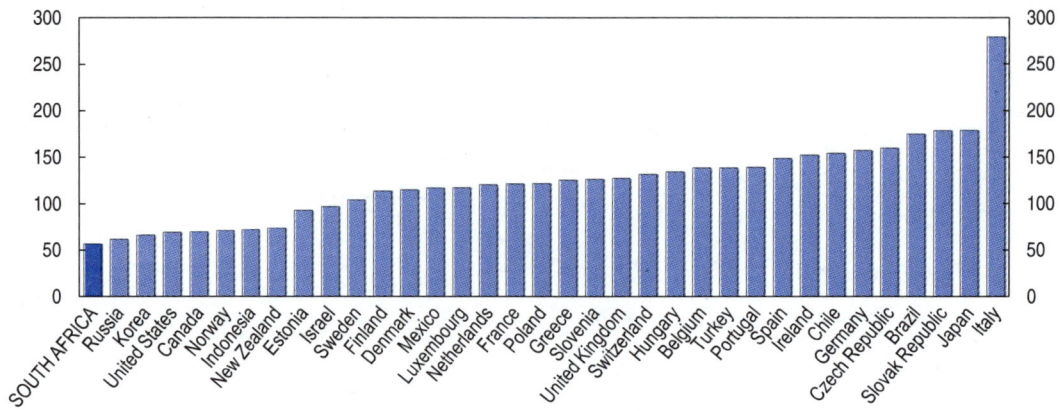

B. Electricity for households

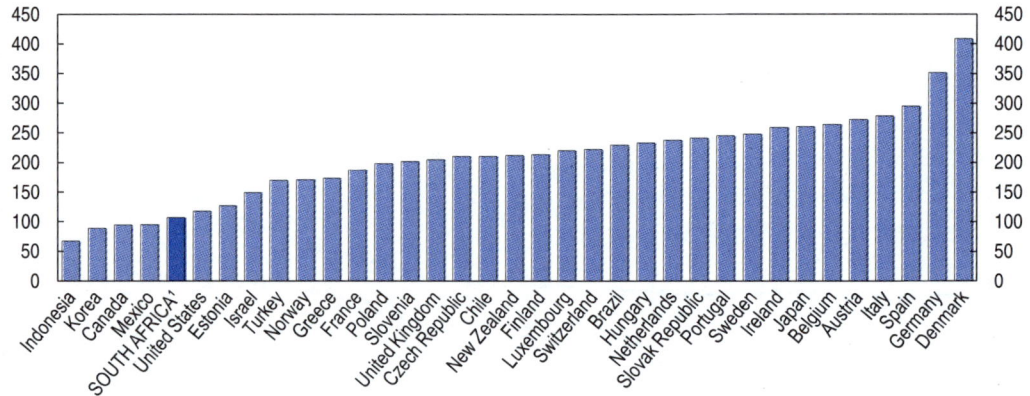

1. Eskom prices for households. Prices set by municipalities are generally higher.
Note: Fiscal year (April 2011-March 2012) for South Africa, 2010 for Korea (industry only), Indonesia, Canada, Estonia and Brazil.
Source: IEA (2012), *Energy Prices and Taxes*; OECD estimates; and Eskom.

StatLink ᠗᠋᠍᠍᠍ http://dx.doi.org/10.1787/888932783572

share of greenhouse gas emissions (both current and cumulative), South Africa's energy intensiveness and heavy reliance on coal impose other costs. Emissions of SO_2 are high by international comparison; in the 2012 *Environmental Protection Index* (EPI, 2012) results South Africa scores even worse on per capita SO_2 emissions than on CO_2 per unit of GDP, ranking 122nd of 132 countries (109th for the CO_2 intensity of GDP). South Africa is also above average for airborne particulate matter (Figure 2.10). Since mining, electricity generation and industry are concentrated in certain regions, the burden of local air pollution is particularly heavy in those areas. Reducing CO_2 emissions would help with reducing the health burden associated with these other air pollutants – about 30 000 life-years are lost each year from premature deaths arising from outdoor air pollution.

The policy response to climate change has gathered momentum

The authorities have shown a growing recognition of the threat of climate change to South Africa and the need for a domestic policy response, as part of a global effort. As early as 1994 a National Committee on Climate Change was established, and a Climate Change

Figure 2.10. **Concentration of particulate matter (PM10)**
Micrograms per m³, 2009

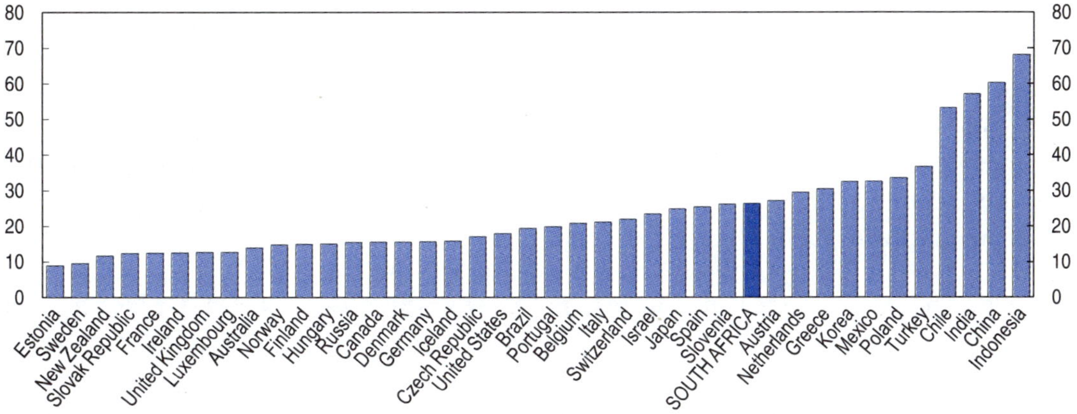

Source: World Bank, WDI Database.

StatLink ⟨⟩ http://dx.doi.org/10.1787/888932783591

Response Strategy was developed in 2004, while in 2003 there were White Papers on renewable energy and energy efficiency. In 2005 a major domestic climate change conference was held and a process created to come up with Long-Term Mitigation Scenarios. The ANC National Conference in 2007 was another important milestone. The ruling party adopted a resolution committing South Africa to playing a leadership role internationally on the environment and to setting a greenhouse gas mitigation target and placing an emphasis on low-carbon technologies for energy production. These commitments were followed up with preparatory work for the COP 15 meeting in Copenhagen.

At the Copenhagen meeting South Africa promised (conditionally) to restrain the growth of greenhouse gas emissions by 34% in 2020 relative to a Business as Usual (BAU) scenario, and by 42% in 2025. The BAU scenario being defined by a range, the commitment amounts to a reduction relative to the upper end of that range. This would allow for an absolute increase in emissions of nearly 30% in 2020 and over 36% in 2025 relative to actual 2010 levels. Per capita emissions would also continue to rise through 2025, though more slowly. As with other developing countries, South Africa made its commitment conditional on the transfer of technology and financial resources from the advanced countries.

The increasing prioritisation of climate change as a policy issue is reflected in further government strategies and policy documents since the COP 16 meeting. These include the 2010 New Growth Path (pursuant to which there was a Green Economy Accord), the Integrated Resource Plan for energy, the National Strategy for Sustainable Development and the White Paper on National Climate Change Response (all approved in 2011, Department of Environmental Affairs and Tourism, 2011), as well as the National Development Plan endorsed by Cabinet in July 2012. South Africa also hosted the COP 17 round of international talks on climate change, which took place in Durban in November 2011.

The White Paper on National Climate Change Response Policy has longer-term projections, going beyond the horizon of the Copenhagen commitment, according to which absolute emissions would be flat from 2025 through 2035 before beginning to decline.

Given continued population growth, per capita emissions would fall by about 1% a year between 2025 and 2035 and somewhat more rapidly thereafter.

Other official targets include the contribution to final energy consumption of 10 000 GWh of renewable energy by 2013 according to the 2003 White Paper on Renewable Energy Policy. This was to be produced mainly from biomass, wind, solar and small-scale hydro energy systems. The Integrated Resource Plan (IRP) builds on this renewables target through 2030, providing for 30% of final energy consumption to be from renewables by the end of that period. The IRP also incorporates a static assumption about energy efficiency gains amounting to about 1% a year through 2020.

The plausibility of the identified targets is under strain given policies in place to date

Taking the degree of ambition on emissions as given, it is not clear that all of the instruments to achieve the objectives have been identified. Given that the bulk of electricity generation will continue to be from burning coal, with several major new coal plants coming on line over the next decade, the emissions intensity of electricity is projected to decline only gradually. This implies a very rapid decrease in emissions-intensity in other sectors, such as transport, if the emissions targets are to be met.

South Africa does not yet have any economy-wide instrument to price carbon, although the electricity levy goes in that direction, since electricity consumption is the most important source of emissions, and the levy exempts electricity production from renewables (though not nuclear). The electricity levy rate is ZAR 0.035 per kWh, which is equivalent to a relatively low carbon price of about ZAR 35 (approximately EUR 3) per tonne of CO_2 (Rennkamp et al., 2012).

The rate of decoupling of emissions from growth, which has been low, would have to accelerate markedly in the period to 2020 for the Copenhagen targets to be met. From 2000 to 2009 emissions from fuel combustion grew by about two thirds the rate of real GDP growth. That ratio would have to fall to about 0.3 in the period 2009-20 in order to stay within the upper bound of the range announced in Copenhagen, and there is a growing recognition that this is unlikely. The National Development Plan notes that the Copenhagen commitment will be missed "without substantial international assistance".

In addition, the set of instruments that has been identified looks to be skewed towards the use of industrial policy to encourage particular sectors as against quickly establishing uniform economy-wide carbon prices that would have a greater potential to influence the behaviour of all producers and consumers (Box 2.2). It is important to recognise administrative capacity constraints, which militate in favour of measures that achieve large effects with relatively few administrative resources. This probably means focussing on electricity (both supply and demand), which accounts for most greenhouse gas emissions, and also argues in favour of concentrating on putting in place a simple carbon tax covering the whole economy. If that is done, it is not clear that there would be significant additional gains from also putting in place a system of carbon budgets, as envisaged in the 2011 White Paper. And there would be less of a case for a range of industrial policy initiatives involving sector-specific assistance.

The multiplicity of plans and initiatives in the area of climate change mitigation suggests a need for a single body to measure and monitor progress vis-à-vis the various targets and to try to ensure coherence between the different initiatives, of only by flagging inconsistencies or disconnects. One model for such a body is the independent Committee

> ### Box 2.2. **Industrial policy interventions to develop the green economy**
>
> In line with objectives articulated in the Industrial Policy Action Plan and the New Growth Path, the government has introduced a range of measures to encourage the development of "green" activities domestically. Prominent examples include the following:
>
> - Renewable Energy Procurement. Local content requirements have been included in the Renewable Energy Independent Power Producer Procurement Programme bidding criteria to encourage the development of local renewable energy equipment manufacturing. Requirements have been incrementally increased in each bid phase. The Green Economy Accord specifies a 35% local procurement target by 2016.
>
> - The Industrial Development Corporation (IDC) Gr-E fund. Renewable energy production and energy efficiency projects are among the qualifying projects for the IDC's Gro-E fund which allocates debt or equity financing of between ZAR 1 million and ZAR 1 billion to businesses at favourable rates.
>
> - The Manufacturing Competitiveness Enhancement Programme. This programme provides grant funding of between 30% and 50% of the total investment cost (with a ceiling of ZAR 50 million) to support "manufacturing and localisation of renewable energy (RE) products and services development". Similar funding is available for a variety of measures that improve the energy efficiency of production (including building retrofitting), make better use of waste products, or promote water efficiency.
>
> - The IDC's Green Energy Efficiency Fund, which provides loans of between ZAR 1 million and ZAR 50 million and preferential rates to firms to fund investments that improve the energy efficiency of their businesses (this includes building retrofitting).

on Climate Change created under the 2008 Climate Change Act in the United Kingdom, but whether South Africa were to follow this approach or use an existing institution such as the Department of Performance Monitoring and Evaluation in the Presidency, it would be best if such a body were accountable to parliament rather than government, in order to ensure that its findings can be publicly debated.

The implementation of the policy instruments that have been identified to meet official targets on emissions has been slow. For example, progress to date on decarbonisation of electricity generation as set out in the Integrated Resource Plan is behind schedule. An important aspect of that process is the contracting with independent power producers for renewables capacity. Following an earlier unsuccessful attempt to set feed-in tariffs to create solar and wind capacity, the process was changed to an innovative series of auctions, with separate allocations for photovoltaic solar (PV), concentrated solar power (CSP), wind, hydro and biomass. The early evidence is that this process does a good job of tracking fast-moving developments in technologies: the price per kilowatt hour for solar PV in the second bid window was about 40% lower than in the first, just a year earlier. But the process has not been entirely smooth. Amid questions about financing for successful bidders, delays in signing contracts following the first two bid windows - the first contracts were signed in November 2012 - have pushed back the timing of the third bid window.

The 2003 White Paper on Renewable Energy Policy set a target of 10 000 GWh of additional renewable energy to contribute to final energy consumption by 2012, to be produced mainly from biomass, wind, solar and small-scale hydro energy systems. So far, only a small fraction of the targeted capacity is in place, and according to U.S. Energy

Information Administration data, total renewables energy production in 2010 was 2.5 terawatt hours (about 1% of total electricity production), which was actually down slightly from 2.7 terawatt hours in 2002. This decline reflects the year-to-year variability of hydroelectric power, which represents the bulk of renewables production to date, but the increase in production from other sources has been negligible so far.

Another source of low-carbon generation in the Integrated Resource Plan is nuclear power, and the plan, finalised just before the Fukushima incident in Japan in March 2011, foresaw an ambitious expansion of nuclear capacity beginning in 2023. With costs and risks perceived to have risen and with timelines strained in the absence of firm commitments, those plans are beginning to look unrealistic and/or excessively costly.

The uncertainty over the nuclear programme also highlights another challenge for the shift to low-carbon generation. The expansion of renewables, while necessary to reduce the carbon-intensity of energy production, also poses major technical challenges to combine base and variable loads. While these challenges can to some degree be met via improvements in grid management, South Africa is likely to need access to additional low-carbon baseload capacity in order to combine achieving the targeted decarbonisation of electricity production and protecting the stability of supply.

The main options for low-carbon baseload capacity are natural gas, probably imported, and hydroelectric power produced elsewhere in southern Africa. Renewable sources combined with energy storage (*e.g.* solar CSP with molten salt heat storage) may also become cost-competitive in time. Options using more regional hydro power and gas were rejected in favour of the "balanced" scenario for the Integrated Resource Plan, in part because of concerns about relying on imported energy. South Africa has a history of prioritising self-sufficiency, from the time of apartheid-era sanctions, and it appears that a relatively high value is still placed on self-reliance.

Security of supply is a valid consideration, given the importance of electricity to the economy, but most OECD countries are heavily reliant on imported fuels, and in some cases significantly dependent on imported electricity. The cost-benefit analysis of price, carbon-intensity and reliability should be regularly reviewed, given the speed of shifts in the global energy picture. For example, the United States is now expected to become a significant exporter of LNG, which could become a cost-effective and lower-carbon competitor for coal. Also, the potential for domestic gas output from hydraulic fracturing ("fracking") is as yet unknown, and its disadvantages in terms of water use and water pollution may turn out to be decisive. If not, however, fracking could go some way to reconciling the preference for low reliance on foreign fuel sources with the objective of reducing the share of coal in electricity generation. In any case, the scheduled regular updates of the IRP should be used to revise it, if necessary substantially, to take into account changes in technology and costs relating to nuclear power, renewables, carbon capture and storage and energy efficiency.

Another area of faltering progress concerns the proposed carbon tax. The National Treasury first circulated a proposal in 2010, but release of a revised proposal, following consultations within and outside the government, has been delayed. Also, when the carbon tax is put in place, it is expected that the initial rate will be set at a very low level, so that it is likely to be several years before the effect on behaviour is significant. There is also a danger of the tax featuring too many exemptions to provide a true economy-wide carbon price.

As against the general impression of a gap between goals and national measures (and particularly implementation of measures), one hope for closing this gap is complementary initiatives at the sub-national level, which could in some cases deliver greater reductions in emissions than counted on in national plans. For example, there appears to be significant scope for small hydro projects in KwaZulu-Natal, while the Western Cape has its own ambitious plans to develop renewables, and has considered imposing its own energy levy.

The relative price of electricity and domestic coal need to rise substantially further

One of the simplest and most important measures is to quickly unwind existing implicit subsidies of coal and electricity. A continued rapid rise in electricity prices is anyway needed to ensure full cost recovery, even excluding environmental externalities. Moreover, the calculations on generation costs reflect assumptions that Eskom will continue to benefit from coal that is much cheaper than the international price. Indeed, the fear that coal will be exported given higher international prices, leaving Eskom unable to get enough coal to maintain electricity production, has led to calls to designate it as a strategic resource, limiting exports. Similarly, the report on state involvement in the mining sector (SIMS) prepared for the ruling ANC recommended that coal be delivered to Eskom on a cost-plus basis, with a limitation on exports (ANC Policy Institute, 2012).

This concern is, however, misplaced and the suggested policy response misguided. National income will be higher if the domestic price of coal is equalised with the export price (adjusting for transport costs). Eskom should pay the market price for coal and the electricity regulator should allow that to be reflected in electricity prices. Only in that way will both Eskom and domestic consumers of electricity have the right incentives to use resources efficiently. As to fears that substantially more expensive electricity will make the tradables sector uncompetitive, it is wrong-headed to seek to protect domestic industry with below-market electricity prices. If domestic tradable goods producers face higher costs as electricity prices rise, creating an incipient disequilibrium in the balance of payments, that should produce a depreciation of the rand, which would maintain balance by switching expenditure from foreign to domestic tradables.

A key aspect of unwinding these implicit subsidies is to ease transport bottlenecks – in rail and ports – which hinder the export of coal. In current circumstances this means more investment by Transnet, but this looks like an example of a lack of competition in network industries leading to worse product market outcomes, underlining the case for reducing entry barriers and splitting up Transnet, as argued in the 2008 OECD *Economic Assessment of South Africa* (OECD, 2008).

Another issue in ending subsidised electricity prices relates to Eskom's below-cost long-term contracts with BHP Billiton for two aluminium smelters in KwaZulu-Natal. The BHP Billiton contracts are not public, but press reports indicate that they deliver electricity at the equivalent of about USD 0.01 per kWh, around one sixth of the average Eskom price and less than half of operating costs (excluding capital costs). Given that the smelters are large consumers of electricity, the implied subsidy is very large. The government has been seeking to renegotiate these contracts, and they were recently referred to the electricity regulator NERSA. It is clearly most unlikely that BHP Billiton would be willing to change the contracts without compensation, but this should be considered, since the most important thing from the perspective of economic efficiency is ensuring that the marginal price facing electricity users reflects both full operating costs (including capital costs) and environmental externalities.

Another aspect of subsidised electricity is the provision of free electricity to poor areas. This is not a major issue for reducing consumption, since in principle only minimal needs of poor households are covered, but in the longer term it would probably be more efficient to achieve the same equity goals via social transfers. The modalities vary by municipality, but overall free electricity is inefficiently targeted – some better-off households receive it while some of the very poor (including, notably, those without electricity connections) do not. It may also aggravate a culture of non-payment for electricity which is already prevalent – Eskom reports that in Soweto (the worst case) only 20% of billed electricity is paid for,[3] and illegal connections are a significant problem in many municipalities.

A faster increase in energy efficiency should be possible

So far, one means that appears to have been underemphasised in South Africa to reduce CO_2 emissions is boosting energy efficiency. The International Energy Agency has estimated that energy efficiency gains, achieved via regulation and carbon pricing, could achieve most of the global emissions reductions necessary to stabilise CO_2 concentrations at moderate levels (IEA, 2009). In South Africa, however, during the period when electricity prices were low and stable the trend increase in energy efficiency was relatively slow by international standards. The energy intensity of GDP declined by 0.9% a year from 2000-09, whereas the average for the other BRIICS countries was 2.6%, and for the OECD 1.5%. For the future, the Integrated Resource Plan is based on the assumption that the trend in energy efficiency gains would be little changed through 2020 before accelerating thereafter as structural changes in the economy increasingly take place.

The main trigger for faster improvements in energy efficiency is likely to be higher energy prices, a factor that was largely absent until relatively recently, and which appears to have been underemphasised in the IRP. The IRP forecast for power output did not factor in any price elasticity of demand – electricity demand was held constant across the different scenarios (which involved different price profiles). The IRP demand forecast is now widely regarded as too high (Rennkamp et al., 2012).

Since 2007, electricity prices have been rising rapidly, providing a test of the responsiveness of demand to the relative price of energy. The real price of electricity (deflated by the CPI) more than doubled between June 2007 and July 2012. Real GDP in the first half of 2012 (seasonally adjusted) was 10.4% higher than in 2007, while electricity output declined by 2.6%. Some of this adjustment is likely to be due to sectoral shifts that are not related to the rising relative price of electricity, but the degree of decoupling in this recent period is nonetheless striking. It is generally considered that short-run demand elasticities are low because structures and equipment are given, whereas long-run elasticities are larger as these factors become variable and as behaviour adjusts. If electricity prices continue to rise rapidly, as they should, there is therefore reason for optimism on meeting official targets on emissions. Whereas emissions rise rapidly throughout the BAU scenario, actual emissions fell in 2009, and electricity consumption, which accounts for most emissions, was still some 2½ per cent lower in 2012 than 2007.

Official scepticism is not always shown towards the effectiveness of price signals in influencing demand. The current proposal for a "standard offer" whereby the state "buys back" unused energy at a premium from firms shows a recognition of the potential for price-based measures. The premium applied is not publicly disclosed, but it may be that the Eskom is, somewhat ironically, the only customer paying fully cost-reflective electricity prices.

Beyond raising energy prices to fully cover operating and capital costs and to properly value externalities, the case for other policy interventions to encourage energy efficiency rests on other forms of market failure. The fact that economic agents are often found not to exploit energy efficiency savings that are privately cost-effective suggests that such market failures are present. The most frequently mentioned examples of such market failures are imperfect information (e.g. lack of knowledge about potential energy savings, leading to under-investment in energy efficiency), split incentive problems (e.g. building owners having little incentive to provide energy efficiency to tenants, who pay heating/electricity bills – this can be compounded by asymmetric information, whereby buyers or renters have less information about energy efficiency than owners) and positive externalities (e.g. demonstration effects of adopting energy efficient technologies or benefits for other firms from research and development).

It is generally accepted that market failures preventing an optimal amount of energy efficiency provide an economic rationale for policy action beyond energy pricing to encourage energy efficiency. Measures commonly used by OECD countries include energy efficiency labels and minimum energy performance standards for appliances, energy performance standards for buildings, energy efficiency reporting requirements for large energy users, mandatory fuel efficiency and CO_2 emissions information for new vehicles, vehicle fuel efficiency standards, and vehicle charges related to fuel efficiency.

Improved spatial planning is another instrument with potential to reduce energy use and carbon emissions, and one which appears to be undervalued in South Africa's 2011 White Paper on Climate Change. OECD research has found that the urban form is a critical factor influencing energy demand and GHG emissions. The *Cities and Climate Change* report (OECD, 2010a) and the 2011 *Regional Outlook* (OECD, 2011d) note that as urban areas become denser and rely on more public transport, walking and cycling, per capita GHG emissions tend to be reduced. Building energy efficiency retrofits are expected to generate significant green employment opportunities in the construction industry (OECD, 2010b). Finally, integrated strategies for transportation and land use planning can generate policy complementarities, including more efficient public service delivery (OECD, 2010c).

At the same time, it is recognised that in general improvements in energy efficiency, particularly when they come from measures that are privately profitable, give rise to "rebound" effects: the increase in income resulting from energy savings generates higher economic activity, which undoes part of the reduction in energy consumption (Jenkins et al., 2011). In the limit, such rebound effects can even result in "backfire", when energy use is higher than before the improvement in energy efficiency. It should be recognised, therefore, that for measures that reduce the price of energy, there may be a limited net impact on energy consumption and CO_2 emissions. This reservation does not, however, apply to energy efficiency driven by higher prices, which is another reason for focussing on that measure.

A number of policy initiatives are already in place in South Africa to encourage energy efficiency. An *Energy Efficiency Strategy* (Department of Energy, 2003) approved by Cabinet in 2005 recognised the considerable scope for energy savings among both firms and households and set out a number of Sector Programmes to encourage energy efficiency. A first review of the *Strategy* in 2008 concluded, however, that progress had been limited, owing to a variety of factors including the lack of a monitoring system to track performance versus targets, the lack of sufficiently strong incentives to ensure improvement of energy efficiency across sectors, the absence of standards for energy management plans and insufficient action to raise awareness of energy efficiency and change behaviour. A second review has been underway since 2011. Recently, the government has also introduced building standards for energy efficiency and approved tax allowances for industrial energy savings, and there are also mandatory standards for electrical appliances similar to those used in the EU. In the aggregate, however, the pace of improvement in energy efficiency seems to have increased significantly only after the beginning of sharp rises in electricity prices.

Cost-benefit analysis is needed to assess other means of reducing emissions

The largest renewables energy initiative to date is the drive to install 1 million solar water heaters by 2014, which is a prominent component of the 2010 New Growth Path and the Green Economy Accord that followed on from it. Installation of solar water heaters is subsidised by around 40%, depending on the model. This initiative has benefits in both environmental and social dimensions, and simple and robust solar water heaters constitute a plausible export industry, especially for export to other African countries. Compared to solar photovoltaic and concentrated solar power, both of which also have potential in South Africa, solar water heating is currently much cheaper. On average, installation of solar water heaters appears to have a payback period of only around 6 years, even without the subsidy, and the cost (private and public combined) per tonne of CO_2 avoided is approximately USD 30 on average, which is much lower than many other renewable energy projects worldwide, although it is higher than the prospective carbon tax would be for many years.

From a static economic efficiency perspective, it would seem better to support renewable energy production in a non-technology-specific manner, with an equal cost per kilogram of emissions avoided. The state of technology in different renewable energy sectors would then determine which are cost-effective. There may be a dynamic case for providing differential support for different technologies, with more support for those at early stages of development in order to allow them to gain critical mass and become cost-competitive. It is not obvious from this point of view, however, that solar water heaters should be singled out for special favour, as the technology used is not notably immature compared to other renewables options.

The other point to make about the solar water heaters programme is that although the economics appear relatively favourable, there is no immediate prospect of this initiative making a large dent in South Africa's greenhouse gas emissions. The target of 1 million installations by 2014 appears likely to be missed by a large margin, and even when it is met, the displacement of demand for electricity would imply a mitigation of only about 2% of South Africa's CO_2 emissions. This highlights the limitations of even large industrial policy interventions in addressing the need for emissions mitigation.

Another technology that is considerably less mature but which may have great long-term potential for reducing emissions is carbon capture and storage (CCS). The economics of CCS remain uncertain, even in advanced economies, and there is no near-term prospect of CCS playing a major role in South Africa's efforts to reduce its greenhouse gas emissions.

On the other hand, South Africa's coal-dependence and geology mean that CCS could make a significant contribution to emissions reductions in South Africa in the long run. In the long-term climate change mitigation scenarios of the IEA CCS becomes a significant factor after 2020 and eventually accounts for over a fifth of the reduction of global emissions where warming is limited to 2 degree Celsius, while for South Africa the contribution of CCS to emissions reduction through 2050 is even greater, at one third (IEA, 2012). One obvious advantage of CCS for South Africa, should it eventually be determined to be cost-effective and safe, is that it would allow the country's endowment of coal to be fully exploited.

The current approach, whereby Eskom is monitoring research in OECD countries and undertaking preliminary geological studies to assess the potential for CCS in South Africa, appears to strike the right balance for now. The move to a carbon tax with significant rates and covering all sectors would be expected to give further impetus to CCS research and development in South Africa. In time, the renewables capacity auctions could include an allocation for CCS.

The introduction of a carbon tax raises design challenges, but simplicity is best at the outset

The National Treasury has proposed introducing a carbon tax, possibly as soon as 2013. The initial discussion document (National Treasury, 2010), argued for a simple tax on the carbon content of fuels, imposed "upstream" to severely limit the number of taxpayers (coal mines, natural gas processing plants, refineries), and covering all sectors. It noted that special relief measures present several difficulties, leading to inefficiency in abatement, as sectors with the highest level of emissions, and hence the greatest scope for abatement, devote socially unproductive resources to lobbying for relief. And it underlined the practical difficulties of using border tax adjustments, including the unresolved question of WTO-compatibility.

By the time of the 2012 Budget, however, the Treasury's proposal had become significantly more complicated than the initial vision. The tax would now be applied on variable percentage thresholds of different sectors' emissions, with the possibility of offsets, and the application of border tax adjustments to exempt exports. The basic tax, before taking into account any special conditions, would apply on the top 40% of an energy user's emissions, at a rate of ZAR 120 per tonne (giving an average tax rate on total emissions, before any exemptions, special relief or border tax adjustments, of about USD 5 per tonne, rising to about USD 10 per tonne by 2020). The later proposal, which appears to reflect the lobbying pressures that the initial discussion document predicted would afflict a more complex tax, would require substantially more information to administer.

A full revised proposal was due to be published during 2012 after further consultation within government and with stakeholders, but remains under discussion. A return to the simpler initial vision of the carbon tax would be advisable. A uniform tax on the carbon content of fuels, applied to all sectors, without border tax adjustments, is likely to be the most efficient instrument to achieve the government's targeted emissions abatement. At the same time, it is true that other countries have also succumbed to pressure to exempt or provide temporary relief to high-emission sectors, thereby diluting the effects of the tax in changing behaviour and putting a greater share of the burden of adjustment on low-emission sectors.

While there may be a case for introducing border tax adjustments to the carbon tax at some stage, in order to ensure a level playing field both in domestic markets and abroad, the advantages of simplicity argue in favour of not including such adjustments initially. With low rates in the first few years, carbon leakage will be a minor issue, and as more jurisdictions move to pricing carbon, the need for border adjustments should decline over time. In any event, as noted in the 2010 discussion paper, differences in technologies within an industry may mean that there is no single adjustment that will correctly compensate all firms in the industry. The informational demands and costs of implementing border tax adjustments efficiently appear formidable, if not insuperable.

Simplicity and sound fiscal principles should also determine what is done as regards the "recycling" of revenues raised from the carbon tax. Earmarking of revenues should be avoided – rather, the extra tax burden should be compensated by a reduction in other taxes. One obvious measure would be to eliminate the electricity levy, which largely acts as a carbon tax for electricity generation. Other tax cuts should be governed by general considerations about efficiency and equity. Given a starting position in which medium-term fiscal consolidation is warranted, tax-shifting need not be revenue neutral; part of carbon tax revenues could be retained to improve the structural balance.

Following through on water policy reforms

South Africa's need for effective water use policies is greater than for most other countries

Increasing access to clean water has been one of the successes of the governments of the democratic era. The 1994 Constitution enshrined access to clean water as a right, and the recent Census indicates that the coverage of basic water supply has expanded greatly, from 59% of the population at the end of Apartheid to 95% in 2011. Sanitation has also improved significantly: according to the WHO/UNICEF Joint Monitoring Programme for Water Supply and Sanitation, the coverage of improved sanitation facilities has increased from 71% in 1990 to 79% in 2010. Unlike much of the rest of sub-Saharan Africa, South Africa will meet the Millennium Development Goal on the provision of clean water.

Notwithstanding the success in improving access to clean water and sanitation to date, there is an acute problem of high and increasing water scarcity, which puts those gains at risk in the future.[4] Among OECD countries only Israel has less available water per capita than South Africa (Figure 2.10). The use of available water resources has risen to over 30% (Figure 2.11), and major water stress is projected to emerge within 15 years, particularly in some inland catchment areas where a large proportion of economic activity takes place. The continued growth of the population and rising incomes will put increasing pressure on scarce water resources, creating policy challenges relating both to ensuring adequate supply and restraining demand. Given that water resources are unevenly distributed, there is likely to be a growing need for intra-catchment transfers, which would imply infrastructure.

The problem of water scarcity globally will be aggravated by climate change, but the impact on semi-arid countries at low latitudes like South Africa is projected to be particularly severe (Intergovernmental Panel on Climate Change, 2007), albeit with considerable variation among regions within the country. Overall, declining surface water availability is likely to be accompanied by a decrease in groundwater recharge. Higher water temperatures, increased variability in precipitation intensity, and longer periods of

Figure 2.11. **Water availability, international comparison**

Total renewable water resources per capita (m³/inhab/yr), 2010

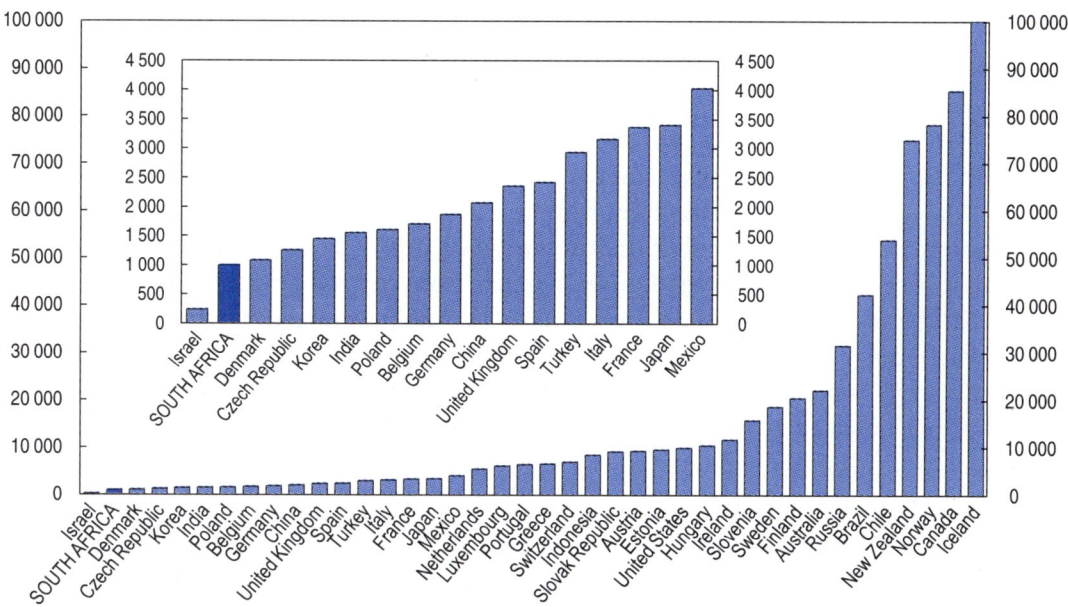

Source: FAO, AQUASTAT Database on line.

StatLink ⎙ http://dx.doi.org/10.1787/888932783610

Figure 2.12. **Pressure on the renewable water resources**

Freshwater withdrawal as % of total actual renewable water resources, latest year available[1]

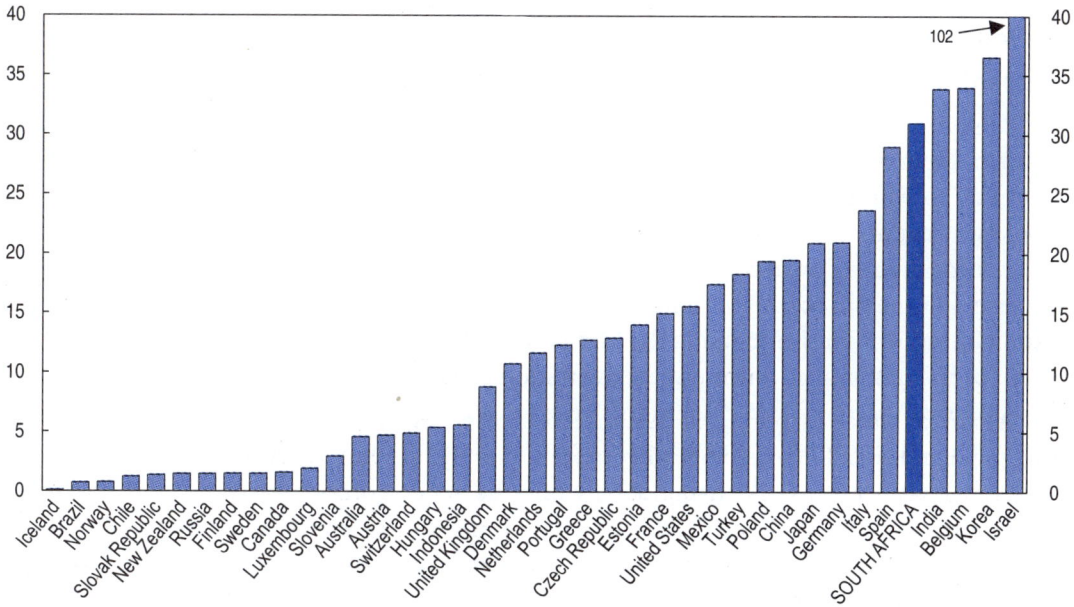

1. 1999 for Luxembourg; 2000 for Chile, Canada, Australia, Austria, Switzerland, Indonesia and Italy; 2001 for Russia
    and Japan; 2002 for New Zealand, Portugal and Korea; 2003 for Turkey; 2004 for Israel; 2005 for Iceland, Finland,
    United States and China; 2006 for Brazil, Norway and United Kingdom; 2007 for Slovak Republic, Sweden, Hungary,
    Greece, Czech Republic, Estonia, France, Germany and Belgium; 2008 for Netherlands, Mexico and Spain; 2009 for
    Slovenia, Denmark and Poland; 2010 for India and South Africa.
Source: FAO, AQUASTAT Database on line and South African authorities.

StatLink ⎙ http://dx.doi.org/10.1787/888932783629

low flows are expected to exacerbate water pollution. Climate change is also projected to increase the frequency of extreme weather events such as droughts and floods and raise the rate of evaporation (Bates *et al.*, 2008).

Moreover, water stress is aggravated by the high water consumption of coal-fired power stations, which will supply the bulk of South Africa's electricity for a long time to come (although the more recent existing plants use less water-intensive cooling technologies, as will the new plants under construction).[5] The OECD *Environmental Outlook to 2050* (OECD, 2012c) presents different climate change scenarios depending on the degree of ambition on emissions reduction. In the "450 Core" scenario for climate change, consistent with limiting the temperature increase from pre-industrial times to 2 degrees, the global reliance on coal-fired power stations is much reduced, which would reduce global water use for electricity generation by 37% relative to the baseline projection. In South Africa, given a much higher initial reliance on coal than the world average, the scope for reductions in water demand from this source is even larger.

One basic challenge for policy is therefore to make water use sustainable. This challenge is heightened by the need to pay due attention to equity. Policy will need to be geared both to restraining overall demand and ensuring that basic needs are met and that the poor are not disadvantaged. Moreover, water management has to be conducted within the context of limited administrative capacity and challenges in governance. Human resources are limited and management structures often fragmented and multi-level governance problematic (Box 1.1), with a mismatch between hydrological boundaries and functional units.

The existing policy framework is based on sound principles, but implementation has lagged

National laws and policies are in line with best practice

Even in advanced countries the use of economic instruments to encourage an efficient use of water and ensure sustainability is relatively recent and evolving. South Africa's basic approach to water management is notably modern and sophisticated, especially for a developing country. It is based on the concept of Integrated Water Resource Management, which aims to take due account of equity, efficiency and ecology. The 1998 National Water Act reversed the previous situation, in which landholders were deemed to own the water resources on their land, and made the Minister of Water Affairs and Forestry the trustee, on behalf of the national government, of the nation's water resources.

A part of water resources is designated as the Reserve, which has two components, ecological and social. The ecological component is the amount of unused water necessary to ensure that water use is sustainable, while the social component is to meet the basic needs of the population. In principle, only when the Reserve is met can other water use be authorised. Such additional water use is divided into Schedule One, corresponding to small quantities of water used for domestic purposes with no probability of negative impacts, General Authorisation, Existing Lawful Use (largely relating to the water use of white farmers in the period before the new law came into effect) and Licenses. It was hoped that the trading of allocations under the licenses would put a price on the marginal use of water and help to ensure an efficient use of this limited resource, once basic needs were met via the Reserve and Schedule One.

In line with best international practice, the government's water strategy enshrines the user pays and polluter pays principles. For urban water, users pay according to increasing block tariffs. An initial block of 6 000 litres per person per month, designed to cover basic needs, is provided free, and thereafter prices rise in steps at successive usage thresholds. This is the same approach used for electricity, and in both cases the price structure rightly charges more for additional use at the margin.

Local government integrated development plans now include a water component; provincial growth and development strategies take into account sectoral development, notably agriculture and conservation; there is a 5-year national water resources strategy; and pathways for sustainability to 2030 have been mapped. Many OECD countries lack a similarly integrated strategy.

The first National Water Resource Strategy (NWRS), produced in 2004, projected that there would be sufficient water to meet all needs in the near future, given careful management. Already at that time, however, allowances for the ecological component of the reserve were not being met in many areas, and the effects of climate change on water availability were not factored into these calculations (Department of Environmental Affairs and Tourism, 2006). Moreover, implementation of the NWRS has lagged, and the system as envisaged is far from fully formed. As the draft second National Water Resource Strategy, circulated for consultation in 2012, admitted, there has so far been limited implementation of Water Conservation and Demand Management; limited implementation of Water Allocation Reform to redress past racial and gender imbalances in access to water for productive uses; inadequate regulation of water resources and compliance monitoring enforcement; a shortage of technical and management skills to implement the National Water Act; poor integration of monitoring and information management; and inadequate establishment of water management institutions and decentralisation of water management.

On the latter front, the authorities have been slow to create Catchment Management Areas (CMAs), which has meant that the planned decentralisation of water management has not happened. The national Department of Water Affairs and Forestry has instead retained direct control in most of the country. Of the 19 catchment areas defined originally, by 2011 CMAs had been created for only 3, and none had been given full licensing powers (Movik and de Jong, 2011). In part to speed up the process of achieving full coverage and to overcome administrative capacity constraints, the number of catchment areas is currently being reduced to 9. The establishment of the CMAs would facilitate the building of local partnerships with water users; co-operation between industrial users and municipalities has already produced demonstrable results, improving wastewater management and reducing municipal water losses.

More monitoring and independent regulation could be useful for urban water supply

The structure of water pricing for urban households is conducive to reconciling efficiency and equity considerations, although in general it appears that average and marginal prices are too low to deliver efficiency. The price per cubic meter is initially zero, rising in bands to a maximum of around ZAR 20 (approximately USD 2.25) per cubic meter, depending on the municipality. The average price for a household consuming 15 cubic meters per month in Cape Town is estimated by the International Benchmarking Network for Water and Sanitation Utilities to be equivalent to USD 0.95 per cubic meter of water, and USD 1.53 per cubic meter for water and wastewater combined. This is much lower than in many OECD countries - Denmark's per unit price is nearly 10 times as high, Australia more than 6 and France more than 5 - but close to the global average and higher than in a few OECD economies.

Although municipalities are formally required to account separately for water services, limitations on administrative capacity mean that this requirement is generally ignored and not enforced. Thus, the information necessary to allow reliable estimates of cost recovery to be made is generally lacking, and improving the data on costs and revenues for the water sector should be a priority. Moreover, there is neither a framework to ensure that pricing is cost-reflective and internalises scarcity, nor clear incentives for municipalities to maximise efficiency and deliver sufficient investment and maintenance. Transfers from the national government are intended to cover the provision of free basic water, while there is also cross-subsidisation among households and between industrial users and households. Municipalities may also use other revenue sources, such as electricity tariffs, to cross-subsidise water supply.

There is little evidence of a generalised financing crisis for urban water supply, although efforts have been made to limit the cost of free basic water provision, which to a significant degree benefits non-poor households. The use of increasing block tariffs appropriately puts a higher price on higher levels of consumption, giving incentives to reduce consumption at the margin, while guaranteeing water supply for basic needs. This is especially so for metropolitan areas, where most water infrastructure (including projects such as the Lesotho Highlands Water Project) is funded by users. Nonetheless, it appears that water is underpriced in at least some areas, leading to underinvestment, poor maintenance and high wastage rates. Other significant problems in cost recovery in urban water supply are non-payment and water losses in transmission.

One reason for the tendency of water to be underpriced in relation to cost recovery needs is political economy pressures to limit tariff increases. While the Water Services Act specifies general principles for the setting of retail tariffs – they are to be cost-based and take into account equity and sustainability considerations, with transparent disclosure of subsidies – little guidance is provided on how to apply these principles in practice, and the water service authorities (municipalities) are self-regulating. Charges are often kept in line with overall inflation in order to maintain affordability and avoid an unfavourable impact on the poor, at least in the short term – however, low water prices (resulting in insufficient cost recovery) often turn out not to be pro-poor, as they tend to result in an undersupply of water services, forcing poor households to buy water from private vendors (OECD, 2012b). In South Africa the free provision of water for basic needs should suffice to protect the poor from higher tariffs in the upper consumption bands.

Given the problems seen in practice to date, and in order to ensure better and more consistent economic regulation of retail water tariffs across the country, there may be a case for creating an independent regulator. An important step towards effective regulation would be to require municipalities (perhaps at first only the largest, metropolitan, municipalities) to properly separate the accounting of costs and revenues for water and sanitation to improve reporting.

The problems of unregulated use and undercharging are greatest in agriculture

As in many countries, most water use in South Africa is for agriculture, and this is where the challenge of ensuring efficient water allocation and limiting water pollution is greatest.

As recognised in the OECD report *Sustainable Management of Water Resources in Agriculture* (OECD, 2010c), there is no one-size-fits all policy for water management for agriculture, but a number of policy directions are generally applicable. In particular, policy-makers should strengthen institutions and property rights for water management in agriculture; ensure charges for water supplied to agriculture at least reflect full supply costs; improve policy integration between agriculture, water, energy and environment policies; enhance agriculture's resilience to climate change and climate variability impacts; and address knowledge and information deficiencies to better guide water resource management.

South Africa still has some distance to go to apply these principles. As regards institutions and property rights, despite the fundamental *de jure* change made in the 1998 Water Management Act, *de facto* little has changed. In part related to the slow progress in establishing Catchment Management Areas, a great deal of agricultural water usage remains unmeasured and uncharged. Very little has yet been done to license agricultural water users, in part because of legal challenges from relatively well-off landowners. Meanwhile, there have been mistakes and inequities. While large-scale farmers were often able to continue using water without restriction, others have sometimes found themselves having to pay for licenses without even having the infrastructure to extract and distribute the water. Companies that run stand-pipes to service poor households that don't have their own water connections have sometimes had to acquire licenses, raising the price paid for basic needs by unconnected households.

Another key issue is the monitoring of water use. There is a National Register of Water Use which contains details of water use registrations, water diversions and waste water discharges, but as recognised in the second National Water Resource Strategy, this register is incomplete and in many cases actual water use is not recorded. A related problem is illegal abstraction of water by farmers from the infrastructure built and paid for by domestic and industrial water users in some areas.

In addition, water charges in agriculture are too low. Agricultural water users, in general, do not pay a return on assets and the depreciation charge is capped. The 2007 Pricing Strategy provides for a 4% return on the depreciated replacement cost of assets, but actual revenue falls far short of this, in large part because most irrigation users are exempted. In practice, therefore, there is still a heavy reliance on the state funding for the operation, maintenance and refurbishment of water resource infrastructure, and this tends to result in underinvestment.

Agricultural water pollution is another significant problem. While the polluter-pays principle is enshrined in law, and while a system for charging for waste discharge was developed nearly a decade ago as an instrument to encourage major polluters to find ways to reduce their impact on the resource, this system has yet to be implemented.

Apart from the crucial issues of measuring and charging for water use at economically efficient rates, including pricing scarcity and pollution, there are other measures to be taken to better manage water in agriculture. In particular, the adoption of drip irrigation and the reuse of effluent and brackish water for irrigation should be encouraged. The National Development Plan proposes a significant expansion in irrigation, with a focus on small farmers and high-value cropping systems, in part via increased efficiencies in existing irrigation, as well as by focusing on areas of the country where there is still surplus water. There may also be a case for taxing fertiliser in order to limit diffuse water pollution, which is hard to measure and charge directly.

Water pollution from mining is a health threat

The problem of acid mine drainage from old disused mines highlights other failures in the tracking and control of groundwater pollution. Acid mine drainage occurs when old mine shafts and tunnels fill up, leading to underground water oxidising. Acid mine water is thought to have been overflowing from the western basin, located below the Krugersdorp-Randfontein area north-west of Johannesburg, for some 10 years. The acid water is believed to be still below the surface of Johannesburg and surrounding areas, but is rising.

The government has taken emergency action to pump out underground water in the West Rand mining basin and to remove heavy metals from the pumped underground mine water prior to it being released to surface water resources. It has also established a Hydrological Monitoring Committee to monitor the quality of mine water in the West, Central and East Rand mining basins, and commissioned a feasibility study for a long-term solution to address the problem of acid mine drainage in the East, Central and West Rand underground mining basins near Johannesburg. Consideration has also been given to an environmental levy, to be paid by operating mines to cover the costs of the legacies of past mining, but no action has yet been taken in that direction, in part because the operators of the old disused mines are not necessarily also current mine operators. While current legislation requires financial provisions to be made for mine closure and rehabilitation, in practice such provisions have been inadequate or poorly implemented, and even the ownership of many closed mines is unknown.

Box 2.3. Recommendations on climate change and water policies

Climate change mitigation

- Reduce implicit and explicit subsidies for energy and coal consumption, and use other instruments, such as cash transfers or supply vouchers, for protecting the poor.
- In designing climate change mitigation policies bear in mind that administrative capacity constraints militate in favour of relatively simple instruments such as a carbon tax.
- Apply the carbon tax as broadly as possible, including the electricity sector.
- Regularly revisit and revise the Integrated Resource Plan to take account of new information about technologies, costs and demand.
- Within the approach to emissions mitigation, increase the emphasis on energy efficiency.
- Give responsibility for monitoring progress on the various objectives relating to climate change to a single institution, and make that institution accountable to parliament via a regular reporting process.

Water

- Accelerate the allocation of water-use licenses and ensure that charges for water reflect supply costs and scarcity.
- Give responsibility for ensuring that water pricing is consistent with national laws and policies to an independent regulator.
- Speedily implement charges for waste discharge.

Notes

1. Actions to mitigate climate change and better manage water resources will not always be complementary, of course. In some cases there are likely to be tradeoffs. For example, the policy of encouraging biofuel production to reduce carbon emissions runs against the imperative to economise on water, since biofuels are relatively water-intensive. And production of natural gas by hydraulic fracturing, which may facilitate a reduction in South Africa's dependence on coal, is also a water-hungry process, apart from possible risks of groundwater pollution.

2. As regards water, it is unfortunate that the draft 2012 National Water Resource Strategy did not include any update on the figures provided in the 2004 Strategy, suggesting that progress in monitoring the use of water resources is lagging.

3. See *IOL Business Report* article of 22 November 2012: "Eskom: Soweto debt stands at R 3.3 bn", *www.iol.co.za/business*.

4. Probably the greatest risk to access to clean water and sanitation, particularly to meet basic needs, is not overall water scarcity but failures of service delivery at municipal level. Nonetheless, increased overall scarcity will sharpen tensions between domestic use on the one hand and agricultural and industrial use on the other, and will tend to make it more expensive to meet the basic water needs of households.

5. Apart from its high water usage, Eskom is cited in the 2011-12 National Environmental Compliance and Enforcement Report as the organ of state with the highest rate of non-compliance with environmental legislation, with several instances of non-compliance with the terms of water use licenses.

Bibliography

ANC Policy Institute (2012), *Maximising the Developmental Impact of the People's Mineral Assets: State Intervention in the Minerals Sector.*

Bates, B. et al. (2008), *Climate Change and Water, Technical Paper of the Intergovernmental Panel on Climate Change*, IPCC Secretariat, Geneva.

Bowen, A. (2012), "'Green' growth, 'green' jobs and labor markets", *World Bank Policy Research Working Papers*, No. 5990, World Bank, Washington, DC, available at *http://econ.worldbank.org/external/default/main?pagePK=64165259&theSitePK=469372&piPK=64165421&menuPK=64166093&entityID=000158349_20120307084323*.

Department of Energy of South Africa (2003), *Energy Efficiency Strategy.* Pretoria.

Department of Environmental Affairs and Tourism (2006), *South Africa Environmental Outlook: Executive Summary and Key Findings.* Pretoria.

Department of Environmental Affairs and Tourism (2011), *White Paper on Climate Change Response Policy.* Pretoria.

EPI (2012), *Environmental Performance Index and Pilot Trend Environmental Performance Index*, *www.epi.yale.edu*.

IEA (2009), *World Energy Outlook*, IEA/OECD Publishing.

IEA (2012), *Energy Technology Perspectives*, IEA/OECD Publishing.

Intergovernmental Panel on Climate Change (2007), *IPCC Fourth Assessment Report: Climate Change 2007.*

Jenkins, Nordhaus and Schellenber (2011), *Energy Emergence: Rebound and Backfire as Emergent Phenomena*, Breakthrough Institute, *http://thebreakthrough.org/blog/Energy_Emergence.pdf*.

Movik, S. and F. de Jong (2011), "License to Control: mplications of Introducing Administrative Water Rights in South Africa", *Law Environment and Development Journal*, Vol. 7/2.

National Treasury (2010), "Reducing Greenhouse Gas Emissions: The Carbon Tax Option", *Discussion Papers for Public Comment*, available at *www.treasury.gov.za/public%20comments/Discussion%20Paper%20Carbon%20Taxes%2081210.pdf*.

Neumayer, E. (2000), "Resource Accounting in Measures of Unsustainability: Challenging the World Bank's Conclusions", *Environmental and Resource Economics*, Vol. 15, pp. 257–278.

National Planning Commission of South Africa (2012), *National Development Plan.* Pretoria.

OECD (2008), *Economic Assessment of South Africa*, OECD Publishing.

OECD (2010a), *Cities and Climate Change*, OECD Publishing.

OECD (2010b), *Cities and Green Growth Conceptual Framework*, OECD Publishing.

OECD (2010c), *Sustainable Management of Water Resources in Agriculture*, OECD Publishing.

OECD (2011a), *Towards Green Growth*, OECD Publishing.

OECD (2011b), *How's Life?*, OECD Publishing.

OECD (2011c), *Towards Green Growth: Monitoring Progress – OECD Indicators*, OECD Publishing.

OECD (2011d), *Regional Outlook*, OECD Publishing.

OECD (2012a), "Monitoring Progress Towards Green Growth: OECD Headline Indicators", unpublished internal OECD document, STD/CSTAT(2012)11STD/CSTAT(2012)11.

OECD (2012b), *The Jobs Potential of a Shift towards a Low-carbon Economy*, Final Report for the Ministry of Human Resources and Skills Development of Canada, OECD Publishing.

OECD (2012c), *OECD Environmental Outlook to 2050*, OECD Publishing.

OECD (2012d), *A Framework for Financing Water Resources Management*, OECD Publishing.

Rennkamp, B., T. Caetano and A. Marquard (2012), "Estimating Effective Carbon Prices: Case Study of South Africa", internal OECD document ENV/EPOC/WPIEEP(2012)8ENV/EPOC/WPIEEP(2012)8.

Stern, J. et al. (2006), *Stern Review: The Economics of Climate Change*, report for the UK Treasury, *www.sternreview.org.uk*.

Stiglitz, J., A. Sen and J.-P. Fitoussi (2009), *Report by the Commission on the Measurement of Economic Performance and Social Progress*, *www.stiglitz-sen-fitoussi.fr*.

ORGANISATION FOR ECONOMIC CO-OPERATION AND DEVELOPMENT

The OECD is a unique forum where governments work together to address the economic, social and environmental challenges of globalisation. The OECD is also at the forefront of efforts to understand and to help governments respond to new developments and concerns, such as corporate governance, the information economy and the challenges of an ageing population. The Organisation provides a setting where governments can compare policy experiences, seek answers to common problems, identify good practice and work to co-ordinate domestic and international policies.

The OECD member countries are: Australia, Austria, Belgium, Canada, Chile, the Czech Republic, Denmark, Estonia, Finland, France, Germany, Greece, Hungary, Iceland, Ireland, Israel, Italy, Japan, Korea, Luxembourg, Mexico, the Netherlands, New Zealand, Norway, Poland, Portugal, the Slovak Republic, Slovenia, Spain, Sweden, Switzerland, Turkey, the United Kingdom and the United States. The European Union takes part in the work of the OECD.

OECD Publishing disseminates widely the results of the Organisation's statistics gathering and research on economic, social and environmental issues, as well as the conventions, guidelines and standards agreed by its members.

OECD PUBLISHING, 2, rue André-Pascal, 75775 PARIS CEDEX 16
(10 2013 02 1 P) ISBN 978-92-64-18230-1 – No. 60441 2013-02